Coloring Outside the Lines

Coloring Outside the Lines

Raising a Smarter Kid by Breaking All the Rules

Roger Schank

HarperCollins*Publishers*

HarperCollins books may be purchased for educational, business, or sales promotional use. For information please write: Special Markets Department, HarperCollins Publishers Inc., 10 East 53rd Street, New York, NY 10022.

FIRST EDITION

Designed by Joy O'Meara

Printed on acid-free paper.

Library of Congress Cataloging-in-Publication Data
Schank, Roger C.
Coloring outside the lines: raising a smarter kid by breaking all the rules / Roger Schank.—1st ed.
    p. cm.
ISBN 0-06-019299-2 02603 4198 5/01
    1. Children—Intelligence levels. 2. Creative ability in children. 3. Child rearing. 4. Education—Parent participation. I. Title
BF432.C48 S33 2000
649'.1—dc21   99-055096

00 01 02 03 04 ◆/HC 10 9 8 7 6 5 4 3

For my kids, and everyone else's kids

Contents

Part 3:
Intervention Tactics

Coloring Outside the Lines

Introduction

I am writing this book because I am horrified by what schools are doing to children. From elementary school to college, educational systems drive the love of learning out of kids and replace it with the "skills" of following rules, working hard, and doing what is expected. They produce students who seem smart because they receive top grades and honors but actually are in learning's neutral gear. They emerge from school and enter careers that are respectable; they may even do reasonably well at their chosen professions. But they are missing something. Some grow up and never find their true calling, diligently working at jobs that are tolerable at best. The effect goes beyond careers, as evidenced by those who lack the intellectual energy to question, to analyze, to innovate, and to take risks. Henry David Thoreau referred to people who lead lives of "quiet desperation," and this term describes those who on the surface may seem to be coping but underneath lack the intellectual development necessary to lead fulfilled, meaningful lives.

These are just my long-term fears about what happens when schools are given the responsibility for raising smarter children. The short-term effects are there for every parent to see. Straight A students are often stressed out from too much homework and too much pressure to maintain their grade point average. While they may become adept at working hard and memorizing facts, they never develop a passion for a subject or follow their own idiosyncratic interest in a topic. Just as alarming, these top students deny themselves the pleasure of play; they don't know how to have fun with their schoolwork or in those rare moments when they have nothing to do.

At the other end of the spectrum, there are the television-addicted, headphone-wearing marginal students. Though they receive mediocre (or worse) grades, they often are just as genetically smart as straight A students. They, however, are not interested in even pretending that they're learning. They've dropped out of school in spirit if not in fact and are lost in a fog of nonthinking activities.

And there are all the kids in between, somewhat stressed out and somewhat bored, B and C students who do the work, don't cause trouble, and are good, middle-of-the-road kids. Their lives may be a bit easier than those of straight A students and they may not waste as much time as marginal ones, but they're no more intellectually alive.

Most kids, in fact, are in the same learning boat regardless of grades and test scores. They lack traits such as inquisitiveness, gumption, and creativity—traits that determine how well they'll do in the real world and how much satisfaction they'll derive from doing it. These are the traits of practical intelligence, and they are what you must nurture in your children.

This book is designed to assist you in this endeavor, providing guidelines and specific suggestions to raise smarter kids, from the time they're born through young adulthood. It will also ground these guidelines and suggestions in learning theory. We all learn in a very specific way, and the method schools use is antithetical to this learning model. As the head of Northwestern University's Institute for the Learning Sciences, I've helped develop and implement this model. I'd like to share with you how I did so and in the process explain how events in my professional and personal life compelled me to write this book.

What I've Learned About Learning, and What You Should Know

I began my academic career with a Ph.D. in linguistics, though my real interest was in how the mind works and how you might get a computer to be smart. In the pre–personal computer era, you needed to use programming language to talk to computers, and it was difficult and annoying; just leaving out a semicolon would cause the computer to have a fit. It struck me that finding a way to help the computer understand English might prove to be a valuable contribution. I was hired by Stanford University as an assistant professor of linguistics and computer science and began pursuing this concept.

From there I went to Yale University, where I set up my own artificial intelligence laboratory, and we had a number of break-through programs, including the development of a computer program that was able to read and understand newspaper stories. Although this attracted worldwide attention and acclaim, I kept thinking about what the computer couldn't do: It was unable to recognize a story it had read before. After reading a story about an earthquake in Iran, why was it unable to recognize a second, third, and fourth story about the same event; why didn't it stop and ask why there were so many earthquakes or figuratively scratch its head and say, "Where have I heard about this before?" I concluded that no matter how smart these programs might seem, they were stupid because they lacked humanlike memories and didn't learn from experience.

It was at this point that my research shifted direction and began to focus on helping computers develop humanlike memories and the ability to learn from experience. To achieve this goal, I needed to better understand how humans learn. Through my observations of people (both children and adults), I saw that they learned based on accumulated experience and not by being programmed with facts. For instance, if you read about an earth-quake in Iran, you first search your memory to see if there is any-thing similar to this event stored there. You then compare the memory to the present event, determine the degree of similarity, and evaluate what generalizations you can make based on this similarity (e.g., Iran sure has a lot of earthquakes). People expect stories to "look" a certain way. When their expectations fail—when there is something unusual or different about the new story—they react with surprise and curiosity, asking questions and wanting to know what went wrong. Clearly, expectation fail-ure is the catalyst for learning. With this principle in mind, we began building smarter computers that would recognize when something was unusual or different from past experiences. The idea was to get computers to experience expectation failure.

At the same time that I was becoming knowledgeable about both human and computer learning, my kids started school. Like many parents, I was frustrated by their problems with the school system—bad teachers, boring classes, rigid attitudes, and so on. Unlike many parents, however, I understood how learning worked. Schools were not offering children a wide enough range of experiences to compare and contrast so they could undergo expectation failure. Instead, their model was built around the memorization of facts, an activity early, stupid computers could perform well. It seemed that the schools could benefit from a new and improved model.

When I arrived at Northwestern University in 1989, I started the Institute for the Learning Sciences to provide schools with the tools to make this new model a reality. My goal was to create great educational software that would allow students to capitalize on basic learning principles. This occurred at a time when per-sonal computers were becoming ubiquitous in schools through-out the country. With the hardware in place, it was just a matter of providing the right software. In theory, this software could transform education throughout the world, creating a pace and level of learning unmatched in history.

While we have been quite successful in translating the theory into some enormously effective pieces of organizational training and educational software, the revolution I had hoped to foment hasn't taken place. It hasn't happened for many reasons, including resistance from educational powers-that-be that have no stake in an educational revolution. School administrators, politicians, and educational publishers are just some of the groups with a vested interest in the current system, and they view any significant change as a threat. While some teachers and a few schools may be following a model that is aligned with how people really learn, most are teaching kids in ways that are remarkably similar to how they were taught a hundred years ago. It's been said that if you took a doctor from 1900 and put him in a modern operating room, he'd be lost, but if you took a teacher from that year and transported her to a contemporary school, she could go to work right away.

I've learned many things in my attempts to work with schools, and first among them is that if parents want to raise smarter kids, they have to take responsibility for this critical task themselves. Not only won't schools do it, but you can't delegate this job to tutors, nannies, or anyone else. I'm not suggesting that you home-school your child—although this is not a terrible idea—but that you take charge of helping your child become a true learner. This has nothing to do with teaching him specific subjects and everything to do with developing the traits characteristic of intelligent, productive, and successful people.

Over the years, I've used my understanding of learning to advise a variety of students and parents in this regard. Adults frequently ask me for help when they have questions about how to deal with the school system, how to teach their children outside of school, and how to choose the right college. I've also counseled many students, as well as the sons and daughters of friends and associates. Based on these experiences, I know what the real issues are and have derived some principles from what I have observed.

While all of us are born with a certain genetic intelligence, we can greatly enhance our ability to achieve and our capacity for learning. I've seen kids achieve and learn far more than most people (e.g., teachers) thought possible based on application of learning principles. My son, Joshua, and my daughter, Hana—both of whom are now in their twenties—were raised using the principles espoused here. Throughout this book, I'll refer to their experiences growing up and how the techniques I used impacted their development. Given their importance to this narrative, I'd like to tell you a little bit about each of them.

Introducing Two Smarter Kids

By the age of four, Hana was reading, and shortly thereafter she began writing her own stories. She was an intellectually active, extremely curious child who loved to learn new things. Then she went to school, where she quickly became stressed and depressed. She hated the teachers' insistence that she sit still and their refusal to answer her many questions. Her feisty nature and strong points of view also didn't sit well with teachers who valued calmness and conformity. Watching her lapse into mediocrity as a student, I decided I would do what I could to preserve her love of learning. This meant that I needed to find ways to stimulate her intellectually outside of school and identify the areas that interested her. As a very bright girl who was very bored and frustrated by school, Hana scraped by with decent grades in most subjects (and indecently low marks in a few of them), eventually graduating from Northwestern. After a few false career starts, she eventually secured a job as a writer and later a software designer at Andersen Consulting, then became involved in writing for the CBS News Web. She then became a Web site designer for a leading ad agency, where she seems to have found her niche. Perhaps Hana would have done as well professionally if I'd abdicated responsibility for raising a smarter kid. I suspect, however, that it would have taken her much longer to achieve what she's already achieved. Despite the best efforts of the school system to brand her as "average" and to demean her intellect, she never thought of herself as anything but a very smart, talented child and never stopped being inquisitive and creative in areas that captured her imagination. Her employers have always found her to be fascinating and original. She is, in fact, a very interesting young adult.

Joshua was a different story. Unlike his older sister, he made an effort to please teachers and radiated goodwill. Initially, his problem was his incredible energy; he couldn't sit still (which his school responded to by taking away his recess privileges, a rather bizarre solution for a child with excessive energy). Later, he was simply bored by school. He had found an area of passionate interest—subway systems—that made his school subjects seem mundane by comparison. He alternated A's one semester with C's the next throughout his school career, applying himself despite his boredom, then allowing it to take over. Still, he tested well and got into Columbia University. He now has a master's degree in air transportation planning from MIT and is pursuing a doctorate at Columbia.

The Obstacles to Raising Smarter Kids in Our Society

Both my children are now doing well in fields they love, but that's not exactly my point. What's more important is that they retained their intellectual energy while all around them kids were losing theirs. They have this wonderful capacity to try new things and be resilient when things don't go according to plan; they may not like failure, but they react to it with questions and exploration, willing to practice something until they get it right. Their stick-to-itiveness when they find something they love will help them achieve their highly ambitious goals, and their insistence on following their own paths (rather than those prescribed by society, parents, or peers) ensures a sense of satisfaction from what they do with their lives.

I'm worried that parents aren't raising their children with these traits in mind. It's not that they don't want their children to lead meaningful, successful lives; it's that more so than ever before, they don't have the time or energy to help them do so. I'm concerned about the recent trends where mothers go back to work months after having babies; where both parents not only work but work long, hard hours and often on weekends; and where children spend more time with baby-sitters, with nannies, and in day care than with a parent. You can't raise a smarter kid if you're not there physically or emotionally.

Part of the problem, too, is that parents don't bother to help their children develop intellectually because they believe their efforts aren't needed and school will suffice. It won't and it doesn't. Let's test my premise in a few different ways. First, how do we learn things? We learn by doing. You learned your job on the job, not through listening to lectures or memorizing facts and figures. When you taught your child to ride a bicycle, you didn't give him a lecture about the mechanics of pedaling or discuss ways in which he might keep his balance. Instead, you put him on the bike, held the handlebars, and let go when he seemed to have the hang of it; he needed to fall, get up, and keep practicing on his own until he became proficient. We all learn through experience, failure, and practice, a learning paradigm that is largely absent from school.

It's unnatural to sit and listen for an hour as a teacher lectures, especially when the subject doesn't interest children; no matter how intently they listen or how copious their notes, their memory of this lecture will quickly fade after they've taken the test. If, on the other hand, they had a conversation about an interesting topic with a teacher and had the opportunity to ask the teacher questions and exchange stories about the topic, they might learn something from this type of dialog. Schools, unfortunately, don't foster these one-on-one exchanges.

Kids need goals to learn, and schools provide artificial goals such as grades or a teacher's approval. As a result, students lack the motivation necessary for their memory to retain what is being taught. If you force a student to memorize the parts of the body, he'll quickly forget them if there's no natural goal behind this activity. If, on the other hand, a student who really is interested in how the body works is allowed to participate in dissecting a corpse and finds the process fascinating, he'll learn the parts of the body more quickly and surely—the knowledge is catalogued more effectively by the brain when it arrives as part of an interesting experience.

There aren't many opportunities for middle school biology students to dissect corpses or run experiments or provide nutrition counseling or hang out in hospitals as assistants or do any of the other things that might foster real learning about biology. And if the schools did provide such opportunities, they would make them part of the curriculum, forcing all students to participate—including the majority who aren't interested in biology or whatever field the school deemed important.

Your job is to do what the school won't do. Identifying your child's area of interest, providing her with experiences related to that interest, and having one-on-one dialogs with her about it are steps every parent can take. As you'll see, you don't have to take an adult education course to nurture the traits that are important to your child's intellectual development.

Reasons for Alarm, Reasons for Hope

You do, however, need to be motivated. Some of you are already sufficiently motivated, having had a number of negative experiences with school or with your child; you want to do something to impact the situation positively. Some of you may need a bit of a push. If so, the following list of warning signs relative to your child's behaviors and attitudes may alert you that a problem exists:

- Lack of identifiable interests (besides television and other nonthinking activities).
- Constant stress related to grades and school.
- Inability to enjoy himself or have fun with any of his school assignments.
- Unwillingness to take risks for fear of failure.
- Refusal to break out of routines, unwillingness to expand her range of experiences.
- Inability to express original thoughts.
- Lack of ambition.
- Difficulty analyzing situations quickly and correctly.
- Tendency to give up easily and not stick with something when things don't go according to plan.
- Inability to think on his feet.
- Failure to ask good, perceptive questions.

You should pay attention not only to warning signs involving your children but to ones involving your own behaviors and attitudes. Take notice if you:

- Infrequently eat meals with your child or take her on trips, to work, or on walks, or engage your child in other one-on-one activities.

- Don't know if your child has a passionate interest or what it might be.
- Spend more time talking to your child than listening to his ideas and stories.
- Constantly pressure your child to work hard and get top grades.
- Routinely dismiss your child's ideas as silly or wrong and tell him to "come back later" when he has something important he wants to ask you.
- Discourage your child from trying something difficult because "he's not ready for it yet."
- Take your child to the same restaurants, on the same vacations, and to the same types of events.
- Place all sorts of restrictions on your child's after school and weekend activities.
- Insist that your child like a certain subject or go into a certain field because it's what *you* like or do.
- Never defend or support your child when he complains about an unfair teacher or a ridiculous homework assignment.

If you're confused by why these are warning signs, you'll soon understand. If you're alarmed because some of them apply to you or your child, don't give up hope. You can change your behaviors and help your child change his. It doesn't take a rocket scientist or a psychologist to raise a smarter child. All it takes is an understanding of how people really learn, a willingness to spend time with your child, and a desire to implement some of the many suggestions you'll find on the following pages.

1

Concepts for Becoming Your Child's Best Teacher

1

What Is a Smarter Kid?

"SMART" is a relative term. School smarts are different from street smarts; the nerdy science genius and the savvy gang leader demonstrate distinctly different abilities, but they are both smart. Or think about where the boundary of intelligence ends and natural talent begins: Was Michael Jordan a smart basketball player or a talented one? It's also instructive to note that some of the most brilliant people do some of the stupidest things. I have a friend who refers to people who are so smart they can't function as suffering from "200 IQ disease."

A book by Howard Gardner called *Multiple Intelligences* proposes that there are myriad forms of intelligence—musical intelligence, athletic intelligence, and so on. In Gardner's view, many people are intelligent in some way, and so the term "intelligence" becomes virtually meaningless. In this politically correct view of intelligence, most of us are smart at something.

Even the educational system's definition of intelligence is relative. Its definition of smart—getting straight A's—is often an indicator of hard work and conformity rather than massive intelligence. We all know students who receive great grades because they are diligent and give teachers what they want; we also know other students who have brain power to spare but receive worse grades because of their indifference, eccentricity, and rebelliousness. While straight A students might actually be quite intelligent, many waste much of their intellect on doing what they're told rather than on exploring their own interests. These people are smart, but they're smart without intellectual passion and original thinking.

"Smart" becomes an even more problematic issue when we factor in genetics. The grand dream of teachers is to take a person who seems hopeless and turn him into a rocket scientist. Or if they can't make that 180-degree transformation, they can at least strive for the more modest goal of taking kids with average intelligence and turning them into college professors. Is this a pipe dream? What about the blue-collar kid with the low IQ who grows up to be a highly successful auto parts entrepreneur? Is he smart about selling auto parts and stupid about everything else?

Given these questions, I would ask that you consider another definition of smart besides the one schools mandate.

Smart Is As Smart Does

Here is what I mean and don't mean by "smarter kid." First, I don't mean you can turn a dummy into an intellectual dynamo. Excuse my bluntness, but it's important to be clear about the issue of genetics. Like it or not, some kids are born with superior intellects. This is just the way things are, and if you happen to have a child who was not blessed with a great mind and you hope this book will turn him into the next Einstein, stop reading now.

If, however, you have a reasonably bright child, then you can help him become smarter by developing six real world abilities:

4

- **Verbal proficiency.** Every parent can help his children learn to speak more convincingly and eloquently. Most kids aren't born with a gift of gab; most aren't destined to be captain of the debate team and a brilliant lecturer. This ability is usually developed, and parents are in the best position to develop it by engaging them in conversation as early and as often as possible.
- **Creativity.** Originality, innovation, out-of-the-box thinking, and other qualities prized in our society aren't conjured out of thin air (or instantly acquired by adults when their employers demand they start thinking out of the box). Parents can encourage creative thinking in kids (or learn to stop discouraging it) by pointing out anomalies, encouraging classification, and taking other, similar steps.
- **Analytical skill.** Contrary to popular opinion (or at least the school's opinion), you don't become a great analyzer by solving lots of math problems. Math does not teach you how to think; it merely teaches you how to do math. If you want your kid to become skilled at sizing up situations and coming to logical conclusions, you need to put him in complex situations and help him work his way out of them.
- **Gumption.** You might also term this ability "stick-to-itiveness." This is a trait highly successful people have in spades, and it's one parents can nurture in their children. Kids who lack gumption are usually humiliated out of it; they're humiliated when they take a risk and fail. By pushing children to speak up and try new and challenging endeavors—and by supporting them even when they mess up—you help them develop gumption.
- **Ambition.** The inner drive to achieve and succeed can be nurtured by parents. Kids who grow up without this drive aren't going to find it by listening to motivational tapes. Parents can instill ambition in their children in various ways, but the overall theme is prompting them to set realistic, meaningful (to themselves) goals.

- **Inquisitiveness.** Curiosity didn't kill the cat, it just made him smarter. The desire and ability to ask good questions about subjects you're interested in is an integral part of being smart. Encouraging kids to explore their ideas—no matter how unusual or strange those ideas might seem—is within the power of all parents. The key here is creating a relationship and an environment in which questioning becomes second nature.

These six traits might not comprise the classic definition of smart, but they are indices of a pragmatic intelligence. Faced with a real world problem, children can use these traits to "originally reason" their way to a solution. To function successfully as adults, your children will find that the ability to originally reason stands them in much better stead than most of the things they're taught in school.

Why Kids Don't Become Smarter in School

Not only do I hope that this book will make your children smarter, but I hope that it helps you stop the schools from making them dumber. As you attempt to imbue your child with inquisitiveness or sharpen her analytical ability, the school system will attempt to thwart your efforts. Not overtly, of course, but in covert, institutionalized ways. It doesn't matter whether you're sending your kid to public or private school, a suburban school or one in the inner city. You need to anticipate and counter the educational system's efforts to dumb your kid down.

Let me give you some examples of what schools do that rob kids of opportunities to develop the six real world abilities, starting with verbal proficiency. Schools hate kids who talk too much or speak out at the "wrong" times. They can't tolerate a child who interrupts a classmate or teacher with an idea she just has to get out of her mouth. Schools have turned "talking out of turn" into a mortal sin. When I was a child, teachers told my parents time and again that I had to learn to stop shouting out the answers in class. It didn't matter that I knew the answer or that I was excited about expressing an opinion. The lesson was: Learn to shut up. This is not a good lesson to teach children in a society where there's such a fierce need for original ideas.

Schools also don't have much tolerance for inquisitive minds. Think of the inquisitive scientist who makes a great discovery. Typically, he pursues his thesis with a single-minded intensity, great resilience (to get past the inevitable failures along the way), and persistence. When schools give children projects to do, however, they discourage this sort of inquisitive pursuit. They set up inflexible time frames in which to complete projects. Children aren't allowed to do things over if they fail or go in the wrong direction. They can't deviate from the assignment, even if they find the assignment boring and want to move in a new direction. This rigid attitude motivates against being inquisitive.

Or think about how schools discourage originality, creativity, and innovation. Curriculum and teacher agendas rarely accommodate students with original points to make. Teachers want the right answers, not the idiosyncratic or unusual ones. Consider how many times you heard a kid ask a "weird" question or say something unexpected in class. The odds are that the teacher responded with "That's interesting, but it's not really related to what we're talking about," or words to that effect. Schools let kids be creative only within narrow parameters. Let's say a student is assigned to write a paper about the themes in *Huckleberry Finn*, and rather than simply writing about the theme of individual freedom versus societal constraints, he devotes most of his essay to the time he ran away from home and the negative and positive aspects of personal freedom when he was on his own. Most teachers would find this approach unacceptable, believing that the student's creativity had taken him too far afield. Far better if he stifles this creative impulse in favor of the expected if boring explication of the book's themes.

This type of anti-creative attitude exists not only in grammar school and high school but in college as well. For instance, I failed the meaning of life in my philosophy class. Until this point, I was receiving an A in the class, a rare occurrence for me. Philosophy was one of the few academic subjects that really intrigued me, and I had read a lot of books in this area on my own. The assigned midterm paper was on the meaning of life, and I had my own distinct philosophy. When I received an F, I confronted the teaching assistant who graded the paper and asked how he could possibly have failed me. After all, isn't one's view of the meaning of life a highly subjective matter? Apparently not. The TA told me my viewpoint was "not the way we're teaching you to look at it."

The trouble with school is that it teaches to the test. The whole process is geared toward memorizing mostly useless facts that are quickly forgotten. Since the six real world skills can't be learned through memorization or measured on a multiple choice test, they're largely excluded from the curriculum.

How We Really Learn

Real learning takes place one-on-one or through self-exploration. In other words, parents rather than the schools are in the best position to facilitate the learning process. Before I give you some ideas about how you can facilitate it, I need to introduce you to two crucial ideas about learning and intelligence: dynamic memory and case-based reasoning.

On a recent plane trip, I was sitting behind two people talking about a training session they had just attended. One of the men noted that there was a lot of material to absorb, and that he was going to have to go home and think about what was taught because he didn't get all of it.

Of course he didn't. That's not the way memory works. Yet all of us who go to school are misled into believing that after listening to a lecture for an hour or longer, we should remember much of what we heard. People with "photographic memories" are considered incredibly smart, at least by the schools. Of course they do well on tests; it's as if they have a crib sheet permanently on display in their heads. But most people don't have photographic memories, and even those who do aren't necessarily smart by any legitimate definition. Being able to remember everything you hear or read doesn't make you more verbal, more analytical, more ambitious, more creative, or more inquisitive, and it certainly doesn't give you more gumption. Still, our society labors under the myth of the mind as tape recorder. The way memory really works is as follows.

Let's say we're having a conversation. When I tell you something, it will trigger objections, ideas, and stories, and you'll want to interrupt me and tell me these things. For instance, I tell you about going to the grocery store and finding that the fruit I bought was rotten. Your mind will process this, which means you'll unconsciously say to yourself, "Where do I have information about rotten fruit?" You go to a section of your mind labeled "grocery store" or to one labeled "fruit." Or you may have a more abstract label such as "people cheating me." Your brain will subconsciously choose one of these places and store what I've told you there. Available in this file are many similar experiences to draw from and with which to compare what I've just told you. These comparisons can take many forms, such as:

"Oh, did you get a rotten banana? That happened to me once."

"Was it at Joe's Grocery store? They have crummy fruit."

"You can never be too careful; I always check fruit out before I purchase it."

The only way for us to understand something is to compare it to something else that resides in our memory. Broken down, the process looks like this:

1. Find the location for the category of thing that happened.
2. Pull that location out.
3. Find a similar situation.
4. Use that similar situation to help process the new situation.
5. Compare and contrast both.
6. Decide what you want to say in response.
7. Decide whether this new experience is worth remembering.

Now let's return to school. The teacher says something interesting during class that triggers this process. Unfortunately, the process is short-circuited because the teacher keeps on talking. You've probably heard people opine, "I don't know what I really think until I talk about it." In most school situations, students aren't allowed to do this. Instead, they have two choices. Either they think about the interesting thing and don't listen to what comes next (which guarantees a bad grade) or they push the interesting thing off to the side and keep listening (in which case they probably won't return to the interesting thing).

So if you want to raise a smarter kid, don't think you can do so by pushing him to memorize facts communicated in lectures or in textbooks. These facts will slide off his brain like a bald tire on ice; there's nothing to hold the facts in place. To help your child create memory "friction," you should place your children in a variety of complex situations. This takes a bit of explaining.

First, consider what's worth knowing. Facts are usually of secondary importance when it comes to accomplishing something.

What's important are skills and cases—the latter term refers to paradigms or rules of thumb formed from our experiences. There are two ways that we can attempt to acquire a skill, as illustrated by the two types of driving tests everyone is required to take. The first type involves memorizing many rules of the road and passing a written test about these rules; the second involves practicing driving a car and then taking a road test, where you have to deal with common driving situations. Memorizing how many car lengths you should keep between your car and another car in order to stop safely will help you pass the written test, but you'll only learn when and how much pressure to put on the brake to stop safely by practicing this skill over and over. Eventually, this becomes unconscious knowledge; you don't have to calculate the car lengths constantly or know the exact amount of pressure in cubic feet you must apply to the brake. You just do it naturally based on your experiences.

So all types of skills (as well as accompanying facts) are learned through doing and practice. But skills are only part of learning; cases are the other part. We establish cases based on impactful direct or indirect experiences. For my generation, Vietnam is a common case, both for people who served there as well as for those who felt strongly about the war. When America invaded Grenada, many people said, "Oh, this is different, because unlike Vietnam, we can get out of there fast." Cases like Vietnam allow us to reason. We frequently use these cases for comparisons or contrasts to other things that happen to us, and they allow us to create exceptions to the case. This is important if we want to think in more complex terms. Rather than assuming that Case A is always true, we come to learn that Case A isn't true in a given situation.

You want your kids to accumulate lots of cases from which to reason and form exceptions. Unfortunately, schools aren't teaching these cases. Children need to experience them in diverse, complex ways, and reading about them in textbooks or listening to lectures about them doesn't work. That doesn't mean we had to serve in Vietnam for it to become a case; it does mean that we had to experience it through protest marches, dorm room debates, nightly news clips, fears of getting drafted, and so on. In other words, a case is anything that has emotional impact on our lives.

Schools should be generating cases through computer simulations, role playing exercises, and innovative field trips. Because they're not, parents need to assume this responsibility. By taking kids on numerous trips and placing them in complex situations, you help them build cases from which they can develop superior reasoning abilities.

I'm Just a Parent; What Can I Do?

Let's start out with something every parent can do: Expose kids to a wide variety of experiences. If you allow your child to fall into television-watching, rock-and-roll-listening, fast-food-eating routines (or any other type of routine), you'll deprive him of the chance to compile cases that will help him reason originally. To keep children from falling into these routines, you have to start introducing them to different, complex experiences at a young age. This means taking them on different vacations each year, having them accompany you to work and seeing you in action, introducing them to a variety of social situations, playing a range of games with them, and giving them challenging puzzles to solve.

This should continue even when they're in high school and college. For instance, when my son and daughter were in college, I strongly encouraged them to join a fraternity and a sorority. The experience of functioning in a large organization—of navigating the politics and policies of such an organization—eventually proved to be valuable.

In planning activities and events for your children, keep the following two criteria in mind:

1. Don't force your child to do things that she dislikes because you think it's something she should learn.
2. Do things with your child that you like, as opposed to pretending to be enthusiastic about it just because your child likes it.

Contrary to what the schools would have you believe, learning should be fun. If learning is force-fed—if you're forced to memorize the periodic tables and you hate science with a passion—you'll quickly forget what you "memorized." That's why it makes no sense to make your child sit through a symphony in a noble if misguided effort at cultural enrichment; she'll get absolutely nothing out of it if she can't stand classical music.

Be alert to what your child does like and shape experiences to dovetail with his interests. When I took my daughter to Europe when she was ten or so, I didn't take her to museums because I knew she had no interest in them. What she loved was visiting castles (not rebuilt castles, I discovered, but only authentic ruins), and so I planned the trip accordingly. When my daughter was twenty-six she took a trip to Belize, where she spent a lot of time visiting the Mayan ruins and loving it.

At the same time, if you hate what your kid likes, don't try to feign enthusiasm for it. I know of one parent who felt that it was important for his child to be "culturally enriched" and so spent a great deal of time (not to mention a small fortune) dragging his son to symphonies, plays, ballets, and art museums. This parent's passion was sports, and he routinely fell asleep in concerts and was bored silly watching most plays. What he should have been doing was taking his kid to football games, but he labored under the misguided notion that his child needed to be drenched in culture. It should come as no surprise that to this day, this child (who is now a young adult) despises theater, ballet, and most of the arts. Even worse, he missed out on many opportunities for experiences that would have been much more meaningful and memorable.

Children are uncanny spotters of phoniness, and if they know you're pretending to like something, the learning experience will be diminished. Your genuine excitement about what you're exposing them to is crucial; they sense that passion, and it helps them become excited about it. For instance, I love to walk. When my children were ages five and eight, they didn't like to walk. Rather than making them go on forced marches, I turned the walks into entertaining outings. I made up games they enjoyed, sang songs with them, and did other things that turned the walks into special treats. As adults, my children love to walk.

The point is to try to expose your kids to things they like, and if they don't like them initially, use your imagination to find ways to make the experiences enjoyable. Sometimes, of course, they will continue to dislike what you love, and you need to respect that. Kids have natural areas of interest, and these are the areas you need to nurture. If an area of interest happens to be something you can't stand, don't pretend otherwise. Fortunately, most children have two parents rather than one, and it's likely that though you might hate an activity, your spouse will like it (or at least won't despise it). One-on-one interactions are better than two-on-one, so hand off this activity to your spouse.

Recognize Your Child's Innate Talent and Encourage It

While a broad range of experiences is important, it's equally important to help children focus and develop their abilities in areas they're passionate about and in which they're gifted. Smarter kids ultimately are focused kids—after they try a lot of things, they start building their experiences in an area (or even a few areas) they're passionate about. Too often, parents expect the schools to recognize and develop their child's gifts. Unless your kid is gifted at Shakespearean analysis or has some other academic-oriented strength, schools are unlikely to identify that talent. Many salespeople, entrepreneurs, professors, and lawyers will tell you that the school system either ignored their skills or misidentified them. Schools are great at determining if someone is highly talented in math or science, but most people with nonacademic (or difficult to measure/quantify) interests and skills fall between the cracks. Even when a child's interest is academic, schools still have difficulty providing a child with experiences beyond a certain range. They may provide a budding math genius with diverse challenges in this field, but they offer him few experiences that allow him to develop his gumption, ambition, or verbal abilities relative to this field. As a parent, you must take responsibility for this job even when your child's interest dovetails perfectly with the subjects he takes in school.

I'm not claiming that this is always an easy job or that you're going to recognize immediately what it is that fascinates your child. With hindsight, I know that both my children gave me clues from a very early age about their interests and ultimate occupations—clues that I missed initially. I picked up on the clues eventually, however, because I started paying better attention to their questions. This is the key:

*If you want to know where your child's talents and interests
lie, pay attention to his questions. The more questions he asks
in a given area, the more likely that's where his passion is and
where his career should be.*

I took my son to Paris at the age of ten and immediately
placed him in a complex situation by giving him a Métro map,
telling him about the Métro, and suggesting he ride it (by
himself). I suspected he'd enjoy it; I just didn't know how much.
He looked at me and said, "Why have you been keeping this
from me?" He rode every single subway line and memorized all
the routes. Then he rode all the Paris bus lines. Two years later I
took him to Brussels and Zurich, and he did the same thing.
When I asked him about his experiences, he excitedly launched
into descriptions of what he saw, drew me maps, and talked about
the subway systems he one day hoped to create. Many years later,
I took him to Tokyo, and it seemed as if he were underground
the entire time. His room was plastered with subway maps, and
for his nineteenth birthday, he wanted nothing more than to ride
a line out in Far Rockaway, New York, that he'd never been on.

When he went to college, he asked me what I thought he
should major in.

"Subways," I said.

"How do you major in subways?"

"I don't know. Figure it out."

He figured it out by becoming an urban planning major.
During the summer, he found a job working in transportation
planning, and then went on to do graduate work in transportation.

Don't discourage your child from following his passion, no
matter how strange or silly it might seem. Certainly I found my
son's early obsession with subways a bit odd. At the same time,
however, I didn't ridicule his interest and in fact found ways to

deepen and broaden it. He knew I was excited about what fascinated him, and that excitement gave him permission to pursue it.

Too often, parents get excited only about good grades and feel
"outside" activities are of secondary importance. I'd suggest
reversing this value system. Paying attention and talking to your
kids about what interests them is the simplest and best thing you
can do if you want them to have more gumption and be more
verbal, more inquisitive, more analytical, more ambitious, and
more creative.

And you can start doing this when children are quite young. In
an elevator recently, I listened to the conversation between a
woman and her two-year-old son. As we rode down, he asked his
mother what the keyhole in the elevator panel was for. She told
him she wasn't sure but that she thought it was a lock for a key; that
people could remove the panel if they needed to fix the buttons on
the panel. They talked about this topic until they reached the
ground floor. Outside, a hailstorm was raging, and the boy pro-
ceeded to ask his mom innumerable questions about the storm, the
size of the hail, the potential dangers of going out in it.

And it struck me that this woman was raising a smarter kid.
When he asked about the keyhole, she didn't reply, "I don't
know," and leave it at that, she didn't yell at him to keep his hands
off it, she didn't make him feel like he had asked a dumb question; she encouraged his interest in the keyhole and then in the
hailstorm.

If there's a model for how to help your small children pursue
their interests and develop expertise in them, this was it.

Identify the Ways in Which Your Child Is Original

The search for signs of original thinking is a worthy quest for a
parent, especially when children are young. Finding the area in

which children express original thoughts is significant. Some kids are original from a verbal standpoint (they say things that are uniquely phrased or unusually perceptive); others are original creatively (they finger-paint amazing designs and images). Think of original as a substitute for smart; it's much more useful for parents to find the area in which their child is original rather than to wait for the schools to determine the area in which he's smart.

Identifying originality in young children can be tricky. For instance, my five-year-old son was at a family gathering where everyone was watching a New York Giants football game on television. In the middle of the game, as the quarterback scrambled around looking for a receiver, my son shouted, "Throw the damn ball, Simms!" Everyone oohed and aahed about how clever he was, how perceptive, how articulate. In fact, all my son was demonstrating by this comment was that he was a good imitator. Children are adept copycats, and my son had heard me rage on many occasions against the irritating tendency of the Giants quarterback to hold on to the ball past the point when reasonable men would throw it.

On the other hand, he did demonstrate originality when watching a different football game in which it was announced that Oklahoma had just beaten Colorado by the unusual score of 82 to 42. I asked my small son how you could score 82 points in a football game. He quickly replied, "Eight touchdowns, eight extra points, and eight field goals, and a safety." He said this while I was still struggling to do the math in my head. This was an example of original thinking in the analytical area; he'd invented his own method of factoring tens to answer my question (while I was dividing by seven).

You need to give children the opportunity to demonstrate their originality because schools usually don't give them that chance. Schools encourage children to follow the rules, to conform, and to avoid doing or saying anything that is provocative or

unusual. The epidemic of attention deficit disorder (ADD) diag-
noses is indicative of the schools' anti-original leanings. I have
friends with bright kids who have had the ADD label slapped on
them, usually because they're unable to sit still for long periods of
times and do project work. The number of hyperactive boys who
have been dosed with Ritalin has become epidemic. If you were
just a little bit paranoid, you might believe that this was a conspiracy among school administrators to drug students into submission.

While some of these children may have problems that need to
be dealt with through drugs and other means, many of them are
simply reacting to the conformity insisted upon by the schools.
Perhaps it's not a bad thing that a kid can't sit for hours on end
listening to one boring lecture after another. Maybe it's a good
sign rather than a bad one when a child is bubbling over with
original ideas and can't keep his mouth shut in class.

My point is that you need to watch for and encourage your
child's originality and not let the schools snuff it out. When children's egos get bound up in how well they do in school—when
they focus all their effort and energy on pleasing teachers and
scoring well on tests—they lose that spark of originality. It's
important to talk to your children about school and grades so
that this doesn't happen. Typically, parents react to their bright
children's problems with school by saying, "What's wrong with
you, you're getting B's, you have to try harder," or "What do you
mean, you'll never need to do logarithms again in your life? You
never know what will be useful when you're older." If you want
to raise a smarter, more original-thinking kid, tell them the truth:

School is a stupid game, but a good college won't accept you
unless you take and do reasonably well on all these math tests
even though you know you want to be a criminal lawyer when
you grow up. So if you want to go to a good school, buckle

*down and get good grades. B's are fine. But don't think for a
moment that your grades have much to do with how smart you
are or how successful you'll be in a career.*

When parents frame school in this manner (and it's framing
that has to be done more than once and reinforced frequently), it
lessens the pressure on children to conform; it gives them permission to be original even if the consequence is a B or an occa-
sional C in a given subject.

School is a formidable foe for parents who want to raise
smarter kids, and as we'll see in the next chapter, parents need to
know what they're up against to fight that foe effectively.

2

What's Wrong
with School?

EVERYONE knows that our schools don't work, though not everyone is willing to admit it. When we look back at our own school experiences through the haze of time, school might not seem that bad. We can recall a supportive teacher or two, an honor won, a rewarding extracurricular activity. What we don't recall is the tedium and the terror, the countless hours spent listening to boring teachers talk about uninteresting subjects or scary teachers humiliating and threatening us into submission. Perhaps cognitive dissonance is the cause of our forgetting: We've spent so much of our lives in school, we figure it must have been worthwhile.

Not necessarily. The movies are a remarkably accurate reflection of what school is really like. In *Gilda Radner Live*, Father Guido Sarducci explains that he's going to open a 5-Minute University that will teach everything in five minutes that students remember after a traditional four-year education. As he notes, after two years of college Spanish all anyone remembers is "Cómo esta usted? Muy bien." In *Peggy Sue Got Married*, Peggy Sue time-travels twenty years into the past when she was a high school senior. Refusing to study for a school math test, Peggy Sue says she doesn't care about it because "I know for a fact I won't need algebra later in my life." In *Monty Python's The Meaning of Life*, a sex education class is being taught not by a lecture but by two naked people making love. Nonetheless, the students are exhibiting "normal" classroom behavior by passing notes, throwing spitballs, and paying little or no attention to the subject at hand. Kids are so conditioned to believe that nothing of interest takes place in school that even when something interesting does take place, they miss it.

For argument's sake, accept the fact that school doesn't make kids smarter and actually makes them dumber. Given that, what can parents do to limit the negative impact of school? You don't need to become an educational revolutionary and reinvent the school system; you don't even have to become an activist and protest at school board meetings. But if you want to raise a smarter kid, you need to do three things:

1. Protect your child against the damage school does and intervene on his behalf.
2. Reassure your child that it's okay if she doesn't excel in school and that there is little relationship between the grades she receives and her intelligence and future career success.
3. Recognize that you and not the schools are in charge of your child's education.

I'll get into how you can do these things later in the chapter. First, you should understand the historical reasons that schools have little to do with making kids smarter and everything to do with making them more obedient.

Creating Docile Factory Workers

In the nineteenth century, public schools were designed to social-
ize children so that they would be good at following orders.
During the Industrial Revolution, there was a tremendous need
for young people to work the assembly lines without asking
questions. School prepared students for this task. The regimentation and standardization of today's schools have roots in the
1800s. The factory owners needed boys and girls who were used
to doing what they were told within specific time frames and
wouldn't speak out of turn.

Today, schools continue these traditions without the excuse of
having to provide workers for the factory. First-graders frequently
arrive at school and shout out answers to questions; they're
excited and eager to explore whatever subject is presented. What
do teachers do when first-graders shout out their ideas? They tell
them to sit down, be quiet, and talk only when called upon. This
makes sense for teachers who want to maintain order and deco-
rum in their classrooms, but it makes no sense from a learning
standpoint. The worst thing you can do to a child with an idea to
express is to tell him to sit down and be quiet. If your child runs
across the living room, tugs on your sleeve, bounces up and
down, and shouts that she has something important to tell you
about her doll, do you say, "Please go away and be quiet. When
I'm ready to cover the subject of dolls, raise your hand and we'll
discuss it"?

Education is terribly tradition-bound. You see it everywhere,
including at college graduations where everyone wears hot,
uncomfortable robes because five hundred years ago all education
took place in unheated medieval halls. We also are burdened by
the tradition of group instruction, which runs counter to our
knowledge that people learn either one-on-one or on their own.
Yet we persist in placing groups of twenty or thirty students in

classrooms with one teacher and expect learning to take place during lectures. Years ago, this may have been the only sensible option. In many towns, teachers were the only educated people around; parents had little or no education and lacked the time or ability to teach their children rudimentary skills like reading and writing. Today, however, most parents are educated, and can spend one-on-one time with their kids.

To do well in this tradition-bound environment, you don't need to be smart; you need to be a grind. Breaking the rules is how you get smarter, and this is frowned upon by educators. A brilliant child may want to design a rocket ship or a Web site, but he's forced to search for the symbolism in *Moby Dick*. If he wants to spend hours in his backyard with his rocket ship, he'll receive a poor grade on his *Moby Dick* test. While there are times when a teacher will recognize a brilliant child and provide the one-on-one instruction needed to let him explore his interest, this usually doesn't happen.

And even when it does, it sets a bad precedent, for it assumes that the only child worthy of one-on-one instruction is the brilliant one. In fact, average students have interests they can explore and become skilled at if given the right type of help. But this isn't the only problem. When tradition rears its ugly head, it is not only a matter of methodology but of content.

What's Worth Teaching

Does a kid become smarter if he can do quadratic equations? Is he smarter if he knows what the green light in *The Great Gatsby* symbolizes? Is he smarter if he can name all the elements in the periodic table? Let's examine some of the subjects taught in school and why they're taught.

Let's start with math. I was a math major and loved the subject, but there's absolutely no reason that anyone needs to be taught anything beyond math basics unless he plans to be an engineer or go into a related field. A misconception exists that to be a doctor or a lawyer, you need to know everything from integral calculus to how to solve differential equations. You don't. I'm a professor of computer science, and most people assume that math would be crucial to what I do. It isn't.

Unfortunately, when schools took hold in the 1800s, math was one of the few subjects teachers knew how to teach. Euclidean geometry was in fashion back then, and understanding geometry seemed like the mark of an educated person. Over time, math became entrenched in the curriculum for a number of reasons, not the least of which is that it can be so easily tested—schools love subjects in which there are objectively right and wrong answers.

There's also the argument that math should be taught because it helps kids learn how to reason. The simple rebuttal to that argument is: Have you ever met a mathematician who was especially good at everyday reasoning? Math professors are notorious for their lack of common sense and logic; they know how to deal with numbers but not with the real world. The better rebuttal is: If reasoning is important (and I believe it is), why not forget math and just teach reasoning? Reasoning is figuring out effective ways to deal with the complex situations one faces in real life, and as such is a highly subjective subject. Unlike math, answers aren't unambiguously right or wrong (which makes it difficult for schools to teach). As a parent, you can and should teach your child to reason early and often. Here are two easy ways to do so:

- **Ask your child's advice for help with problems you're having in your life.** For instance, a neighbor is irritating you with his loud music and you don't know how to bring this issue up to him. Or you're faced with a difficult business decision and you don't know if you should choose Solution A or B. Give your child the chance to reason out a plan of action with you.

- **Encourage your child to reason out her own problems.** Ask her to list next week's activities, prioritize which ones are worth doing first, and plan a schedule to accomplish her goals.

Literature is another unnecessary subject. Yes, kids need to know how to read. No, they don't have to read Dickens, Tolstoy, Shakespeare, and others in the "canon." Reading great works of literature does not make you smarter, nor does it provide the much-hallowed "common ground," as E. D. Hirsch of *Cultural Literacy* fame contends. Hirsch believes that there are certain things kids and adults should know; there are certain authors who are indispensable to maintaining our cultural standards. If everyone hasn't read *Red Badge of Courage*, for instance, we would all be worse off because we would lack a common basis for discussion. In fact, the common things people talk about—who won the big game, which celebrity just got divorced, the latest White House scandal—aren't taught in school. We have plenty of cultural commonalties, and nineteenth-century books aren't one of them, except for a small group of intellectuals and literature professors.

Then there's the argument that reading great works of literature elevates children's minds and helps them develop an aesthetic sense. That's true only if the books are germane to a child's life. It's difficult for a fourteen-year-old to appreciate the beauty of a Shakespearean sonnet if he views it as an artifact of Elizabethan England and can't see its relevance to the issues he's facing in his relationships. You can force children to read books, compel them to talk about the issues the books raise and write the proper words about these books on essay tests. But none of this is internalized, and it is forgotten as quickly as it is "learned." Ideally, fourteen-year-olds should read books about other fourteen-year-olds. Or books about adults who they imagine they might some-day become or situations similar to those they might find themselves in.

Schools should allow each kid in a class to read a different book—a book that that specific child is excited about. The assignment would be for each child to excite his classmates about his particular choice. They could engage in one-on-one discussions with each other, write their feelings about the book for others to read, and so on. The literary qualities of the book as well as the issues it raised would stick in a child's mind far better than a book chosen because it's a classic and taught through tests and teacher-led "discussions" (where teachers do more lecturing and explaining and students do less discussing). Of course, this ideal scenario rarely happens because it requires teachers to do a great deal of extra work. More significantly, this scenario is unlikely because it's difficult to test children when they're all working in an highly individual manner.

As a parent, ask your children to read books if *the books are about something that matters to them.* When my daughter was eight, I gave her a book to read about how a child survived the Holocaust. It was an adult book and not easy to read, but she made her way through it. As a Jewish child, she found the story relevant to her life, and she found my excitement about the book to be contagious. My son, on the other hand, who was interested in reading only sports-related books, would not have had the same reaction. This was fine. Each child is different, and to have your own, predetermined canon of books you want them to read is as silly as the schools expecting every student to enjoy and appreciate *Billy Budd*.

Then there's writing. Asking children to write an essay on what they did on their summer vacation is a classic assignment.

It's also one that bores children to tears, as evidenced by the uninspired essays teachers usually receive about "going to the beach" and "meeting new friends at camp." Kids write what teachers want, not what they feel about the topic. When asked to write an essay about the theme of man versus nature in *Moby Dick*, most students will feed teachers the words they expect they want to hear. When there's no involvement in the writing, no learning takes place.

My daughter loved to write, but she often ran into obstacles when she had writing assignments in school. In eighth grade, for instance, she always received B's on her papers. It turned out that the kids who received A's structured their essays in a way that the teacher favored. When my daughter adapted her writing style to fit this accepted structure, she too received an A. Shortly thereafter, she decided that the "A" approach was boring and reverted to her old style, willing to sacrifice top grades by doing so.

What I did was to reassure my daughter that her teachers weren't the world's leading authorities on writing. I also encouraged her to write the way she wanted to write, regardless of the grade she received. Every parent can do these two things and take some of the trauma out of bad grades in a subject kids care about. These actions also make it easier for kids to maintain their integrity and interest in writing. If kids love aliens and writing, encourage them to write a story about what might happen if aliens took over their school or landed in the neighborhood. Or have them keep a journal about a trip the family takes and distribute copies of it to relatives. While I wouldn't recommend giving a kid who didn't like writing such an assignment, I think it's great for children who hunger for chances to write about what they're interested in.

You might also encourage them to write for the school newspaper or literary magazine. In these publications, there's much less direction from teachers about what to write, and students can write about topics that have more relevance to their own lives. In fact, it would be great if the majority of writing kids do in school was for student newspapers and magazines, with kids constantly reporting, commenting, and reflecting on things that were important to them. Unfortunately, this type of writing is often viewed as far less important than composing essays about *Silas Marner* or writing poems in strict iambic pentameter. It's not that essay writing is unimportant; this is a skill that anyone who aspires to be a writer should learn. But if a student has absolutely zero interest in an essay topic, he can't possibly be learning anything. A bright kid might receive an A on an essay he does virtually by rote or even cleverly "borrow" the opinions of critics who have written on this subject and plug them into the school's acceptable essay structure. But unless he is engaged by this novel, the only thing this experience teaches is how to get a good grade without doing much original thinking. Now, if someone truly hated *Silas Marner* and were allowed to write a critical essay about why it was a complete waste of time and all copies of the book should be burned, then that might be a good learning experience. This student would use his analytical and creative abilities to craft a convincing essay; he'd actually care about coming up with original points and revising a sentence or section that failed to support his thesis. Most students, however, would be reluctant to write this type of essay, knowing that most teachers would give them a poor or failing grade for "not taking the assignment seriously."

History (usually taught as "social studies") is certainly a valuable subject for people to understand, if for no other reason than the oft-cited admonition that those who ignore history are condemned to repeat it. At the very least, democracies need intelligent voters. Unfortunately, our educational system doesn't produce enough smart voters, which is why political debates rarely revolve around substantive issues. Part of the problem is that what a twelve-year-old learns about imperialism is largely irrelevant at this point in his life. By the time he's an adult and can join the public debate and vote on foreign policy, he will have forgotten everything about Manifest Destiny and the mistakes made in Vietnam. The larger problem, however, is the way in which history is taught. If history were made relevant to twelve-year-olds, the lessons might stick with them. The problem is that complex, ambiguous, multifaceted subjects are boiled down to a few words on a multiple choice test. History is not learned by regurgitating correct answers. It's not learned through memorizing dates of famous battles. It's about putting kids in situations where they have to reason out complex issues and solve problems faced by people throughout history. Role playing and gamelike situations would be a much better way to teach the subject. Kids could take on the roles of our Founding Fathers and have a debate about amendments regarding free speech and gun control; they could play war games in which one group represents Napoleon and his advisers while the other consists of the British military figures trying to defeat him.

Now let's speak of languages and why foreign languages are infrequently spoken in our classrooms. In most foreign language classes in the United States, an inordinate amount of time is spent on learning grammatical rules, vocabulary words, and customs of a given country. When kids do talk in a foreign language, it usually is a result of raising their hands to answer questions. This is not real conversation. People learn foreign languages through one-on-one dialogs, and this should be the focus of study from first or second grade. All we need to do is provide kids with a bit of coaching and an opportunity to hear a language and speak it frequently. If a child can learn English, it's likely he can also learn Spanish and become fluent in it if he's introduced to it early in life and given the chance to speak and practice it frequently.

Finally, there's science. The essence of science is creating a hypothesis and then trying to prove it's right. Science teachers rarely allow students to create their own hypothesis and try to prove it. Instead, they lecture about the different parts of matter and the scientific names of plants and expect kids to memorize difficult words. Nothing sticks because these names are irrelevant to most kids. What's relevant to most kids are three scientific subjects: nutrition, health, and reproduction. This should be the core of the science curriculum in schools (perhaps with electives in chemistry, physics, etc., for those kids whose interests reside in these areas). In addition, science should be taught as a "doing" subject. Field trips, lab experiments, and the like are ways to involve kids in testing their own hypotheses. Some kids will have their own hypotheses about why the lake near their homes can no longer support fish. Let them try to pollute water in a fishbowl using different materials and determine which chemicals are responsible for polluting a nearby lake. This is as opposed to most lab and field work in schools, where kids are trying to prove someone else's hypothesis or conduct experiments in which they already know the correct outcomes.

The Six Traits of Smarter Kids: What You Can Do That the Schools Can't (or Won't)

It's not just that the schools teach the wrong subjects or teach the right subjects the wrong way. It's not only the structure and environment of the schools that fails to foster learning. The trouble is that the six traits that children need to become high-functioning, successful adults—the real world definition of smart—are frequently ignored.

In the last chapter, we touched on a few ways this is so. Here, let's look at each trait in greater detail and explore how you can help imbue your child with each trait in ways the schools cannot.

Verbal Proficiency

When kids talk in class, they're not talking about things they're interested in or in ways that are natural (that represent the way they talk with friends and family). Instead of a real one-on-one discussion, children are asked to raise their hands to provide short answers to factual questions. When a child is assigned a topic to present to the class, he is urged or required to outline his talk and rely on notes. Many children simply give presentations by reading what they've already written. The same things happen when classroom debates are held. Students do a great deal of research on assigned topics and are asked to argue pro or con positions regardless of how they really feel about the issues involved.

Verbal ability is about thinking on your feet. It's about repartee. It's about quickly coming up with responses, retorts, and ideas and expressing them in clever and convincing ways. In life, unlike in school, you rarely have notes. When my son was going to give his first presentation in school, I recommended that he do it without an artificial aid. It was scary, certainly, but over time it helped him develop a facility with thoughts and words.

If you want to help your child become more verbal, here are two simple things you can do:

- **Make sure your child has something to say every night at dinner.** Encourage him to report on what happened during the day. Have him describe something that was funny, sad, or hurtful. Clearly communicate that it's not acceptable for him to sit there in brooding silence or to mumble into his food. Dinner table conversation should be just as important as eating.
- **Challenge what your child tells you.** Parents have a tendency to accept what their kids say at face value. They're unwilling or uninterested in saying things like "What do you mean by that?" or "How can that be?" or "That doesn't

make any sense; explain what happened in more detail." You don't have to be mean about it, but you should put your children on the verbal defensive. Don't allow them to make an outrageous statement without supporting it or an inaccurate one without thinking twice about it.

Creativity

When I use the term "creativity," I'm not referring to being "artsy." Being creative is not a talent confined to one of the arts. It is possible for an individual to be creative if he's a businessperson, car salesman, or scientist, or in some other profession not automatically associated with creativity. I was invited to serve on a New York Festival of the Arts panel that consisted of prominent people from both the arts and the sciences (seating was done alphabetically, and I was seated between Hal Prince and Stephen Sondheim). At a certain point in the discussion, the moderator said, "Now let's hear what *the creative folks* have to say about this," referring to Prince, Sondheim, and their artistic brethren. The moderator's inference was that the scientists on the panel weren't creative. Nothing could be further from the truth—at least the truth that will help parents raise more creative kids.

Schools view creativity just as this panel moderator did. They assume they're fostering creativity by exposing students to the arts. While it's certainly possible to be creative in the arts, forcing a child to play the tuba for two years in middle school won't translate into creativity in other areas of his life.

A while back I wrote a book called *The Creative Attitude*. In it, I defined creativity as a willingness to come up with and pursue one hundred ideas knowing that ninety-nine of them are stupid. If you examine the history of creative and inventive people, you'll find that almost all of them had ninety-nine dumb ideas before they hit on one great concept. The creative attitude is having the chutzpah not to be defeated by naysayers who put down your ideas. In other words, you need to keep plugging away.

Schools (and the workplace, for that matter) don't encourage kids to voice and experiment with all their ideas. When kids receive verbal criticism from teachers and bad grades or barbed remarks from fellow students, it shuts down their creativity. Parents can counter this effect by encouraging children to pursue whatever odd and doomed-to-fail notions they may have. Be prepared for a lot of wacky ideas. No matter how strange they might be, don't discourage your child by calling his idea "weird" or "wrong." If he is dead set on building a toy house from blocks that you know is going to fall down, don't say, "This isn't going to work." Get down on the floor, help him, and when the house does fall down, encourage him to try a different approach. When he sees that nothing awful happens when his idea fails, he'll be willing to try again. This is the source of true creativity.

Analytical Ability

Schools attempt to teach analysis when they ask students to explain why a character in a novel took a certain action or what factors caused a war. They think their goal is to teach literature or history, when in fact what's really important is not the curriculum subject but the analytical process. When you ask a child who hates math to analyze a story problem and he struggles to work out the right answer, what he's really thinking is: "I don't care." Motivation is crucial to developing analytical abilities, and there's not much motivation in most school assignments. If, on the other hand, a teacher were to ask students to analyze who is going to win the NBA championship or who is the best Spice Girl, they would be motivated to analyze these situations. Real learning takes place when motivation is present. People learn from their mistakes in logic only when it's important for them to get it right. Only then does the analytical process they learn stay with them.

If you want your children to develop their analytical skills, give them assignments that are relevant to their lives, such as:

- List the five reasons why some kids don't have as many friends as they'd like to have.
- Explain why you don't want to do your chores and why you shouldn't be required to do them.

Unlike an analysis of the causes of the War of the Roses, these exercises will prompt most kids to analyze with gusto.

Gumption

Smarter kids possess a stick-to-itiveness that helps them achieve amazing things. Gumption isn't genetic; it's learned. Some kids refuse to quit; they are stubbornly and aggressively persistent. This doesn't happen because of what they've been taught in school. In fact, school teaches children to quit. The highly competitive, stressful nature of school creates a winner-take-all atmosphere. Only one kid can be quarterback, valedictorian, or captain of the debate team. For every activity and in every class, teachers foster a sense of intense competition where the grinds prevail. For many kids, all that work and the lack of fun doesn't seem worth it, and they quit.

If you want your children to develop gumption, encourage them to keep working at something they care about no matter how many times they fail at it. This may seem obvious, but many parents are quick either to criticize ("You're never going to do it *that* way") or to let the child quit out of a false sense of compassion ("You've been out there long enough trying to build it; come on in"). Schools usually don't allow children to retake tests when they get C's. A C is considered average and therefore acceptable. But there are no C's in life. You either succeed or fail. What schools should do is give children the option of retaking tests until they receive an A. That might encourage gumption. My son decided that he wanted to be a baseball pitcher, and at a young age he began practicing this skill by throwing a ball against our backyard fence. For three years he threw the ball until the fence finally fell down. For me, it was certainly worth the cost of a new fence. He kept throwing that ball day after day, and lo and behold, he became a pitcher on his high school baseball team.

That he didn't become a college or professional pitcher is irrelevant. What he learned was that if he kept at something long and hard enough, he'd do well at it. He learned the value of gumption, and he learned it without becoming a grind. To him, throwing the ball against the fence was fun. Gumption and fun aren't mutually exclusive; in fact, they go hand-in-hand. If the schools were in charge of making my son a pitcher, they would have filled the process with competition, stress, and precious little fun. Gumption isn't about being the very best at what you're interested in. It's about being persistent and enjoying what you're being persistent about.

Ambition

Ambition has two components, and school teaches neither one of them well. Or rather, the educational system's concept of ambition is quite limited. Simply put, it involves getting all A's, going to Harvard, and obtaining a high-paying job. I believe ambition should evolve from a student's passionate interest. My mother considered only three professions worth pursuing: doctor, lawyer, or engineer. Since I knew I didn't want to be a doctor or a lawyer, I started out as an engineering major. When I ask college students what they want to be, a large percentage of them tell me that they want to be lawyers. Most of them have only a vague idea of what it's really like to be a lawyer, and it is fostered primarily by television. Schools do an absurdly poor job of educating students about professional possibilities. Guidance counselors have little grasp of career paths and lack the skill required to connect a student's interests with various careers. And of course, schools rarely offer students the chance to visit actual workplaces and experience firsthand what they're like.

This is where parents can have an impact. The popular "take your daughter/son to work" day is the right idea, but it's executed in the wrong way—one day watching you work is insufficient. If your child expresses an interest in law, for instance, he should visit a variety of legal workplaces—the district attorney's office, a corporate law firm, and a legal aid clinic. Suggest that he secure a summer internship at one of these places. Perhaps he can volunteer after school somewhere else. All this will direct your child's ambition; it will give him something meaningful to be passionate about.

But ambition shouldn't be limited to just work. Kids can be ambitious about doing things in the community, about being parents themselves, about their relationships with others. A parent can broaden his child's definition of accomplishment by communicating his pride in the child's willingness to stand up to a neighborhood bully or to help a kid who's new to the neighborhood. In school, accomplishment is measured by grades and awards. Outside school, it can be measured by a sense of self.

Inquisitiveness

Kids are born inquisitive. Even the dullest of babies explores his crib, stares at his hand, and is fascinated by lights. Teachers, however, discourage this quality from day one in the classroom. Whether or not teachers are willing to admit it, their greatest fear is that they'll be asked a question they don't know how to answer. They've positioned themselves as authority figures with all the answers, and as a result communicate to their students that any question off the subject is not appreciated. When they tell a student, "Good question!" it's because they know the answer to it and it fits with the day's discussion.

You can restore your children's natural inquisitiveness by doing the following:

Encourage your child to ask questions but don't answer them.

This is not as strange as it sounds. For instance, my teenage son asked me, "Why is Southeast Asian food so spicy?" I told him this was a good question and he had enough information to figure out the answer himself. He groused about my response but took the challenge, played around with the information in his head, and eventually arrived at the correct conclusion: Asian food is spicy because Asian countries are in hot climates where food spoils quickly and spices are used as a preservative.

Visits to unusual places—a new Asian restaurant, for instance—encourage kids to ask questions. Trips to new cities and countries, provocative books and movies, and anything that is unusual and unexpected triggers questions. If your child asks a question to which she really wants to know the answer, she'll usually be willing to search for that answer on her own. When she looks things up on the Internet, reads books about a subject, and asks more questions, her natural inquisitiveness is restored. The problem with television, of course, is that it inherently answers all questions and doesn't raise any.

All School Is Bad, But High School Is the Worst

As you attempt to help your child become smarter in ways the schools won't or can't, you'll encounter different challenges at different grade levels. As a general rule, college will be the easiest because students are given a certain amount of freedom to pursue their true areas of interest. Certainly elementary school is difficult because children are facing thorny socialization issues, and middle school makes kids start to sweat by demanding they bring home good grades in boring subjects. But at least the former provides students with a certain amount of doing activities that are fun and the latter has a certain amount of curriculum flexibility and innovation.

High school, however, is a nightmare. This is where the maniacal emphasis on standardized tests, rigid course requirements, and grades reaches its apogee. State curriculum committees, textbook publishers, and the Educational Testing Service conspire to maintain the status quo. The result is that every high school student is taking the same basic courses as every other high school student. If every kid had the same interests, this would be fine. But because every kid has his own unique interests, this core curriculum is anathema to true learning. Not only that, but the competitive pressures and stress build throughout the high school years and reach unmanageable levels for many students.

Parents often tell me that they know their children are under too much pressure and that they recognize that many of the courses they're taking are irrelevant to their lives. But they add, "I want my child to get into a good college, and I also don't want him to be a lazy goof-off and develop bad habits."

Certainly you have to set a few limits. You don't want your child to receive consistently poor or failing grades in *every* subject or to become a discipline problem. But you can help reduce some of the stress he's under and give him a greater opportunity to be smart in the subject he wants to be smart in by doing the following three things:

- **Communicate to your child that you care about only one grade.** Tell her something to this effect: "I'm not particularly concerned if you bring home B's in most of your subjects or even if you receive C's in one or two of them. What I do care about is that you bring home one A per semester in the subject you really like." So many parents (especially high-achieving professionals) have their egos wrapped up in their child's grades; they worry about having to tell friends and relatives why their son or daughter didn't make the honor roll or didn't get into a top school. Being smart isn't about competition, at least based on how I define smart. It's about falling in love with a subject and being intellectually curious about it. If you're a grind and get into a top school without having this intellectual passion, you'll go nowhere (except maybe to a therapist for a Prozac prescription).

- **Don't allow your child to become a homework machine.** From a learning theory perspective, homework is a great idea. It says to a child: "You should do this on your own and you're capable of doing it on your own." Remember, we learn only on our own or one-on-one, and homework is an opportunity to explore, to make mistakes and discoveries. Unfortunately, the majority of homework students receive is in subjects that don't interest them or consists of assignments that make an interesting subject boring. Kids receive tons of homework at earlier and earlier ages, coming home from school and having precious little time for anything else. As a result, they don't have time for their own independent projects—homework they assign themselves that they really want to do. Give your children permission and encouragement to pursue these independent projects, even if means they have to rush through homework and do a less than stellar job on it.
- **Defend your child against oppressive teachers.** This is probably both the easiest and the most difficult action a

parent can take on behalf of a child. It's difficult because most of us give teachers rather than our own children the benefit of the doubt; we assume that if a kid is having problems with a teacher, something must be wrong with the kid. In fact, the opposite is usually true. There are too many mean, small-minded, vindictive teachers in the school system. Just about everyone has had teachers who tortured students with sarcasm, insults, and massive amounts of homework, creating classroom environments that were better suited to Pavlovian obedience than to learning. If you determine that this is the case, your job is easy. Get your kid out of the classrooms of these sadistic teachers. Talk to the offending teacher and the principal, put your complaints in writing, threaten to involve other parents. If you raise a stink, you can usually protect your child by moving her out of a classroom or making sure the teacher knows he's going to have to deal with a parent out for blood if he continues this behavior.

Perhaps the best way for you to deal with the school system is to think of yourself as a professor with clout. If things aren't going well for your child at school, you have the power to intervene. Assume that you are an eminent authority in charge of your child's education. The best models for schools are Ph.D. programs at universities. This is one-on-one education at its best, where professors guide graduate students, helping them pursue research on topics that the students have chosen and find fascinating. Rather than lecturing and forcing them to take multiple choice tests, these professors ask provocative questions, suggest different directions, provide feedback, and serve as sounding boards for the students' ideas.

You can do exactly the same thing for your child.

3

Getting Started

PARENTS frequently feel powerless when it comes to their child's intellectual development. Caught between the school system and the genetic hand their child has been dealt, they often feel as if they can't do much beyond encouraging their kids to study and get good grades. This fatalistic resignation that dominates parental attitudes and actions assumes that teacher knows best and that even if the teacher doesn't, kids will achieve what they've been "programmed" to achieve.

Throughout this book, I'll provide various tools and techniques for parents who want to have an impact on their child's learning and growth. Many of these are designed to achieve specific goals or to deal with specific problems or opportunities every child faces. Here, however, I want to arm you with some basic strategies that can benefit your son or daughter enormously. They're relatively easy to implement, are applicable to everyone, and create an environment in which real learning can take place. As you'll see, they lay the foundation for raising a smarter kid.

Set Yourself Up As a Fair but Firm Authority Figure

Children don't learn much from parents who are martinets or pushovers. The former make learning a terrifying experience and the latter lack the authority necessary to get kids to believe what they tell them. There is a middle, higher ground that parents should strive to occupy.

You need to establish discipline and set rules but also be willing to negotiate these rules. When my daughter was two, I took her to a toy store and told her that she was allowed to choose only two toys. Toy stores, as every parent knows, cause children to erupt in hysterics. To avoid these hysterics, I told my daughter that if she started crying, she wouldn't get any toys. Less than a minute after we entered the store, she was hugging four toys and refused to give up any of them, hysterically crying that she wanted all of them. I told her that she had violated our deal by crying and that she wouldn't receive any toys. Suddenly she sucked up all her tears and said in a tremulous voice, "I'm not crying now." I renegotiated our deal and allowed her to pick one toy.

This taught my daughter that rules are rules but that you can try to reason with the rule-maker. Over time, I set many rules and I tried to be consistent in the way I enforced them. Though I would bend the rules in response to a reasonable argument, I was careful not to do things that would render them meaningless. Kids being kids, they're going to test the rules constantly. By being consistent in their enforcement, you let them know that you're not some bubble-headed bozo who doesn't mean what he says. You become someone whose ideas and opinions are worth considering.

Schedule Alone Time

My kids went to bed earlier than any of their friends until just before they reached adolescence. This might not sound like a way to lay the foundation for becoming smarter, but that's exactly what it was. This rule in our house ensured that they'd wake up early (usually around 5:30 A.M.) when my wife and I were still sleeping. They were not allowed to wake us up, but they were encouraged to do anything they wanted (except watch television). This gave them a few hours to themselves each day, and during this time they were tremendously inventive. Unable to call friends or play in a group, my children were left to their own devices. My son, who became an urban planner, drew cities. My daughter, who has worked as a professional writer, read books. Though they sometimes played together and acted out wildly imaginative scenarios, they often played on their own. While you can schedule alone time at any hour, it tends to work better when children are fresh and alert after a good night's sleep rather than when they're tired and cranky at the end of the day.

Alone time is when children learn to be self-reliant and creative. It allows them to fill up with original ideas. No matter what their interests are or the professional paths they eventually take, being alone provides invaluable sustenance for their minds. If you want kids to develop traits such as ambition, inquisitiveness, and gumption, make sure they have some time by themselves each day. The seeds of these traits aren't planted or allowed to flourish if children are constantly watching television, listening to rock music, or playing electronic games.

Kids need quiet to think and focus. You would assume that most parents would recognize this simple truth. Instead, they are often terrified when they catch their children doing nothing. "What's the matter with you, don't you have anything to do?" the parents ask the child who is just sitting there. "Why don't you call a friend?" they urge. If they bring their child with them to an adult party, they also bring a video so that they can talk to their adult friends and their child (and perhaps other children) won't be bored or bother them. This teaches children a terrible lesson: Being pacified is the key issue in life, and being a watcher is a state worth aspiring to.

Children are not alone when they're watching television by themselves. They're accompanied by an invisible teacher who communicates negative messages. Most sitcoms teach that life is silly and that you can turn everything into a joke. Most dramatic series teach that treating people shabbily and casual nastiness are standard operating procedure. Commercials are even worse, teaching kids that lying can be an art form (slickly manipulative commercials show viewers that if they use their product, they'll be beautiful, rich, successful).

It's easy to take potshots at television, and I'm certainly not the first one to do it. It's a ubiquitous presence in just about every home, and I recognize it's difficult to stop children from watching it. But if you want to limit its deleterious effect on your child's mind and provide him with an extra hour or two by himself, follow these simple suggestions:

1. Severely limit the amount of television your children watch until the age of twelve or so; their protests won't be so vehement when they're younger and you'll be able to give them precious alone time when they really need it.
2. Control what and how much they watch when they're twelve and older. There's a growing feeling in our society that teenagers should be allowed to make their own choices and live with the consequences, that it's unfair to impose adult values on adolescents. I've heard parents attacked for censorship because they won't let their kids watch certain shows. This is nonsense. If you want to raise a smarter kid,

you need to set boundaries, and one area in which you must set limits involves television. Talk to your children in advance about what they want to watch, decide if it's okay, but don't let them watch more than an hour a night. There will be some brain cells destroyed, perhaps, but you're exercising reasonable damage control.

3. Help your children recognize that they're smart and special. Television preys on kids who feel uninteresting and average; it represents an escape not only from their bland world but from what they perceive as their bland selves. Telling your child she's special is fine, but you also want to demonstrate that fact repeatedly and starting at an early age. I remember making a videotape of my daughter when she was eight, and on the tape she said she was the smartest girl in her class. "How do you know?" I asked. She said, "I just am." She knew she was the smartest because I had demonstrated to her in a variety of ways that she was. When she was little, I bought her a book called *Girls Can Be Anything*. It reinforced her notion that she might be the first woman president when she grew up—a notion I had planted in her mind. Imbuing your child with a noble ambition can become a self-fulfilling prophecy. Whether my daughter was actually the smartest kid in her class is irrelevant. What matters is that she believed she was smart and had the qualities necessary to be president. Give kids a sense of their uniqueness and special qualities, and give them time by themselves to fantasize about these things. This will "entertain" them far better than any television show.

Start Teaching Before Your Child Reaches School Age

There's this widespread notion that kids possess a limited ability to learn until they're old enough to go to school; that they can't really do or absorb much beyond playing with toys, drawing stick figures, and listening to simple stories. As a result, parents aren't particularly ambitious or adventurous when it comes to teaching their children because they figure they haven't developed a "real" capacity to learn. In reality, we all possess this capacity from the time we're born.

For instance, you can have your kids reading by age three or four. This is important not only because it will give your child a head start in school, but because it will help him develop a love of reading. Schools teach reading in groups; you can teach it one-on-one and tailor the reading to your child's interests. In other words, you can make the experience fun and highly personalized as opposed to the by-the-numbers, impersonal approach created in the classroom setting.

In addition, getting kids to read at an early age gives them something worthwhile to do with their alone time. Self-learning is the best and most important form of learning, and reading is a good way to develop this habit. For this reason, it's not that important what children read, as long as it interests them. Don't be concerned if your child reads only sports books or fairy tales or every children's book ever written on birds. The act of reading is what's important; any type of reading increases vocabulary and range of experience.

If you want your child to read early and often, here are some suggestions.

First, it helps if you love to read and your children observe the pleasure it brings you. If you read a lot, they'll attempt to mimic your behavior.

Second, make reading a warm, fuzzy experience. When they're babies and toddlers, put them on your lap and read them a book. Point at the pictures, do funny voices, entertain them.

Third, get some magnetized letters to put on the refrigerator and start with three-letter combinations. Let your kids play with them, arranging and rearranging the letters. Encourage them to pronounce the three-letter combinations. When they master those, gradually increase the difficulty. By the age of three or four, you should be able to have your child reading using this method.

Fourth, when your child is able to read, take him to the library and let him choose his books. While you should guide his choices, let him pick. Even at this early age, kids learn best when they have the freedom to choose a subject that interests them.

Fifth, when your child is a bit older and has found an area of reading interest, raise the bar. Give him a challenging book, even one that may seem beyond his abilities. The odds are that your child will struggle his way through it (demonstrating our desirable trait of gumption), asking you questions when he becomes stuck.

I know many parents who decide not to teach their children to read because they think the schools have some magic method and that if they interfere, they'll somehow mess up their child's ability to read. Or they worry that if they do succeed in teaching their children to read, the kids will be too advanced when they finally start school and will be bored with the classes.

Of course they're going to be bored if they're smarter kids. Be prepared for it. Your child may also shout out the answers or ask the teacher challenging questions because you've helped bring out her inquisitiveness and gumption. Or she may daydream during class in response to this inherently boring experience. Take it as a positive sign if this behavior happens.

Besides teaching your kids to read, you can do other things to help them develop intellectually before school starts. "Why" is a word little kids say frequently. They're bursting with questions, and you need to give them all sorts of opportunities to ask them. When my daughter was four, we hiked up to the top of a mountain, sat down, and gazed out at the landscape below. I told her that now we were going to philosophize. She asked me what that meant, and I told her it involved looking at the world and asking why it exists: where did the people, the birds, and the trees come from. She asked why a lot during this conversation, but philosophize she did. When she started school, experiences such as this one enabled her to skip a grade and made her excited about learning.

The point of this is to encourage children to become excited about learning before school whittles away their passion for all things new.

Don't depend on nursery school to instill this excitement. Some parents expect nursery school to prime the learning pump and therefore refrain from taking on this responsibility themselves. What nursery school actually does is teach children their colors as well as other intuitive lessons. Nursery schools don't want to cover the same ground that will be covered in first grade, so even though most children are ready to learn all the first-grade subjects at least a year or two earlier, nursery schools opt not to teach them. While it's true that at three years of age, many children might not sit quietly in a classroom and listen to a teacher talk about more significant subjects, you don't have that problem as a parent. Because you're doing one-on-one teaching, you don't have to worry about where you do your teaching or if your child speaks out of turn. If you wish, you can teach philosophy on the top of a mountain.

Nurture Connected Relationships

You can't raise a smarter kid if you're not available to do so. Two-career families—especially two-career families where both parents have inflexible schedules and are gone all day and travel a great deal—will have difficulty doing some of the things I'm suggesting. If neither parent is around much, the child won't develop the connectedness necessary for learning. The educational paradigm I believe in is based on failure, and if parents are largely absent, kids won't have the parental connection that makes failure an experience with which they feel comfortable. Let me explain how this works.

Children are natural failure machines. They're perfectly willing as toddlers to try to walk, fall down, and try to walk again. They also don't mind speaking nonsense words in their effort to communicate, and they'll keep speaking gibberish until they get the words right. A parent who is usually available provides reassurance and an emotional safety net for their mistakes, encouraging children to try again. A parent who is often gone can't provide this support, nor can a parent who complains, "Can't you do anything right?" or mocks their mistakes. Kids whose failures are criticized or not supported become risk-averse. They don't ask questions or try new things. Assuming they'll be yelled at or receive some other sort of negative message if they fail, they'll simply do things that are familiar and safe.

Learning takes place when people fail at something they're interested in, ask questions about it, fail again, ask more questions, and persist in doing it until they get it right. An exploratory learner is willing to take risks and fail, and he is willing to do so because he has a safety net: you. As a parent, you pick your child up when he fails, pat him on the back, and encourage him to fail again. Instead of criticizing his failure, you provide emotional support and help him figure out what he did wrong.

My son called me from MIT one evening when he was a graduate student. He told me all the lights had gone off in his apartment, and he didn't know how to get them to go back on. I asked him if there was a circuit breaker box, and he said no, there was a box, but inside there were "little glass things." Fuses, I explained. I suggested that if he looked at one of the fuses, he'd see that one of them had "burned" and that the fuse burns out so the apartment building won't. I then explained how to replace the fuse. Now, my son should have been able to figure this out, even though he'd never lived in a place with fuses before. No doubt he was embarrassed to ask his question about the fuses to anyone else for fear of seeming dumb and inexperienced. But he was willing to ask me. Knowing that I wouldn't yell at him for asking a stupid question allowed him to take this risk. The connectedness that allows him to ask me any question is what I'm advocating.

It's unlikely that kids will achieve this connectedness with anyone but a parent. Perhaps there's a rare teacher who can connect with a student in this way, but it's probably you or no one. In school, teachers are constantly judging and downgrading failure. There's lots of disconnection taking place.

At any age, we all have an impulse to establish connectedness with a teacher. As adults, we do so with religious figures, gurus, coaches, and mentors. Finding this type of special relationship facilitates both one-on-one learning and self-learning—the only types of learning that mean anything. As a parent, you can establish this connectedness in a variety of ways. Though I was working when my kids were growing up, my schedule was flexible enough that I could be home a significant amount of time. When they came home from school, I tried to be there. One day my daughter asked me a question right after school, and we explored the answer together. Afterward she said, "I'll be back when I need you again." Being there at the moment kids "need you again" is one way to establish connectedness.

You'll also recall my earlier advice about not feigning interest in an activity because your child is interested in it (or you want him to be). Your child knows you better than you think, and sooner or later she'll recognize that you're deceiving her. This diminishes the trust and ultimately the connectedness between the two of you, making her unwilling to fail in front of you. Remember that learning is an emotional experience, not just a "pure" cognitive one. If you love something, kids will sense it and respond to it. I love football. From the time my son was tiny, I did football-related things with him: took him to games, threw him passes, talked about strategy. When we watched the Giants together when he was two, he used to jump on my lap when the Giants scored a touchdown. He was too young to really care if the Giants scored, but he was old enough to know that I would be receptive to his jumping on me when they did. Throughout the years, football has established a connection between us. At the same time, it's been the source of a great deal of incidental learning—the strategy of psyching out opponents, competing hard, planning ahead—that translates to other aspects of life.

You can establish connections with children in different ways and at different ages. I cannot overemphasize the value of a one-on-one trip in this regard. Traveling somewhere new and different with your child is a highly versatile learning experience (and I'll examine the range of ways your child can benefit from this experience in other chapters). It is something that has worked for me as well as for other people to whom I've recommended this technique. This isn't a family vacation with Mom, Dad, the kids, and the dog. It's one parent and one child going somewhere by themselves. When I took my daughter to see the ruined castles in England, it was just the two of us. There was time and opportunity for her to talk about what was on her mind, and it made her feel special and important. More to the point, it helped us establish a bond that proved critical for her self-education.

Make the Most of Your Child's Questions

Some parents don't have time for their kids' questions or dismiss them as stupid or inconsequential. Other parents take great pains to answer every question in detail, giving mini-lectures in response to queries. Neither of these approaches fosters learning.

Here's Schank's paradox of childhood learning:

> *The worst thing you can do is not answer a child's question,*
> *and the second worst thing you can do is answer it.*

When children ask questions, they're expressing interest in a subject and setting the stage for a true teachable moment. If the question is really meaningful to your child, you should drop everything to address it. But if you answer it directly, you destroy the possibility of exploratory learning. If you respond pedantically and offer a mini-lecture that bores her to tears, you run the risk of flicking the learning switch off in her mind.

Most children (and most people in general) don't ask questions to receive answers. They ask them because they're intrigued, puzzled, and provoked. They want the chance to bounce ideas off an expert, to get some guidance so they can find the answer themselves. This is especially true when children ask open-ended questions ("Why do we die?" "Why do birds have wings and we don't?"), but it's also true when they ask factual questions. Let's say your child asks you what Brazil's major export is. A good response would be: "Well, what do you think it is?" Your kid may not like that response at first—he might tell you that if he knew what it was he wouldn't have asked—but if you're patient and give him some hints, he'll pick up the ball. You might ask him what he knows about Brazil's climate; you might talk to him about Brazil's jungles. Eventually, he'll start making some guesses based on the information he knows, and the odds are that he'll figure out the right answer or at least be sufficiently motivated to look it up.

Over time, this approach facilitates self-learning; it convinces kids that the answers they need are often inside rather than outside, that they can figure them out for themselves.

The key to knowing how to respond to your child's questions is being intimately aware of your child's frame of reference. People learn best when they compare a current situation to a past experience. If your child is having problems with X, you can help him recall the time he dealt successfully with X-prime. When my son was at summer camp for the first time, I went to visit him on parents' day. When I was about to leave, he began to cry, telling me he was sad. I asked him if he had ever experienced a situation similar to this before. After some prompting, I helped him recall how four weeks earlier he had been sad in the same way when he got on the bus to go to camp. "How long did it take you before you stopped feeling sad?" I asked him. He said it took about a minute before he met someone he liked on the bus, started talking to him, and forgot all about being sad. He brightened as the comparative memory worked its magic.

To answer many of your child's questions—especially before he's a teenager—will require that you know him well. When he's tearing his hair out trying to read a difficult book or do a difficult math assignment, you can remind him of a similar assignment that he completed successfully in the past. But you can remind him of it only if you know that it happened.

Consider the Following "What Do I Do If . . . ?" Questions

When I talk to parents about these issues and the simple things they can do to raise a smarter kid, they invariably ask me a question that begins with, "What do I do if . . . ?" or something along these lines. The following are the six most commonly asked questions and my responses:

1. What do I do if my child isn't very good at something? What do I tell him? Should I pretend that he's good as a way of encouraging him?

Be honest with your children. By helping them understand what they're not good at, you indirectly point them toward something they can be good at. I can't tell you how many kitchens and offices I've walked into that contain a child's dismal attempts at drawing. The parents gush over their child's stick figure man or blobs of finger paint—"Isn't this great?"—and I'm forced to reply, "No, it's pretty awful." Kids are resilient (though some parents aren't). They're aware that their finger-painted boat looks nothing like a boat and they can take a critical review in stride. It does much more harm than good to tell a kid that her crummy painting would make Picasso weep with envy. Kids know when you're blowing smoke. You need your child to believe you no matter what and not to wonder if you're being honest.

2. What do I do if my kid's interests are dumb, silly, or off-putting?

Support your child's interests even if you don't think very much of them. Most interests can be "expanded" into careers, no matter how mundane or juvenile they appear early on. The child who loves computer games may become a software designer. The child who spends hours listening to heavy metal music may become a sound engineer. The child who plays obsessively with Lego blocks may become an architect. As a parent, you can gently prod him in the areas he's interested in. Suggest things to do that might be a little more challenging than what he would otherwise choose. Get him to stretch himself. Like it or not, this interest area is where your child will probably earn his living one day. It is far preferable to push him forward rather than hold him back.

3. What do I do if I don't have time to do the things you're suggesting? Can't a qualified nanny be as effective, and if not, can't lessons accomplish these same goals?

Remember, learning takes place individually or one-on-one. Lessons usually entail groups, and when you're part of a group, your individuality is often devalued. You have to behave in certain ways, conform to norms, and sacrifice your particular interest for the common good of the group. Nonetheless, we live in a time when parents are bombarding their children with group lessons of every conceivable type. While private lessons are better, the instructor lacks the vested emotional interest of a parent. Without a stake in the outcome, an instructor frequently teaches according to a script rather than responding to the individual needs and interests of the child. Using a nanny or grandparent or someone else as a surrogate teacher-parent often doesn't work. While there are some grandparents (and perhaps even some nannies) who have extremely close relationships with children, most don't. As a parent, you have a unique relationship to your child, a bond of trust and intimacy that's difficult for others to duplicate. So if you really want to raise a smarter kid, make the time.

4. What can I do to get my kids thinking and exercising their minds rather than just sitting there listening to CDs or playing video games?

Play nonelectronic games with them. The dinner table and car rides are great places to play simple games with your children. I used to give my kids quizzes at the dinner table, and the prize was different types of desserts. I used to ask them questions that required them to know useless facts, like who was the third president of the United States. The winner might receive six pretzels, the loser only two. Both my children loved to shout out the answers. The point of this game wasn't to teach my children trivial facts but to have them practice thinking fast and competitively.

5. What sorts of conversations should I be having with my child to help her acquire the learning skills you talk about?

You should be having arguments. Not knock-down, drag-out arguments, but fun, challenging debates. When your child says one thing, take the opposite position. Play devil's advocate. Test her assumptions. If you want to raise a verbal kid who thinks on her feet, you'll argue with her. Your role is that of a classic Talmudic scholar. You should not be antagonistic but argue with a twinkle in your eye. The novelist Joseph Heller, in *Good As Gold*, provides a number of exchanges between a father and his son that capture this dialectic. Here's an excerpt from one of them (p. 105):

> "So how come," said Julius Gold, "you work for him, and he don't work for you?"
>
> Now Gold understood. "I don't work for him. I'm a freelance writer. He's an editor."
>
> His father appeared ominously pleased. "Did you write this or did he?"
>
> "I did."
>
> "Did he pay you or did you pay him?"
>
> "He paid me."
>
> "That sounds like work to me," said his father with sovereign scorn. "Do you wish you was him, or do you wish you was you?"
>
> "I wish I was me."
>
> "Does he wish he was him, or does he wish he was you?"

Conversation is the lifeblood of learning. Talk to your children at every opportunity. When they point to things before they can talk, explain what it is they're pointing at. When they're just learning how to speak, play "dialog games" with them. I taught my daughter to talk and get dressed by herself simultaneously. When she'd get up at the crack of dawn, I'd still be lying in bed half-asleep. When she'd come into the room, I'd tell her to get dressed. "Get a shirt," I'd say. She'd come back with a pair of pants. "That's not a shirt, that's pants," I'd explain, and then add, "Go get a blue shirt." She'd come back with a red one, and I'd tell it was red, not blue. She learned to talk and dress herself by sixteen months.

6. My child has a high IQ, so do I really have to work that hard as a parent to raise a smarter kid?

No question, some kids are born with great intelligence. Genetics counts. On the other hand, I've seen many very bright kids ruined by parents and schools. If you're a parent who spends little time with your bright kid or forces him to pursue something he's not interested in, you've squandered his genetic inheritance. Force a child who is passionate about ska music to become a lawyer and you've produced a dumb lawyer. If you use the television as a baby-sitter, rarely challenge your child's statements, always praise whatever he does, and never use your child's questions as an opportunity to explore ideas, then you won't raise a smart kid. He might do well in school, but he won't be creative, have gumption, or be verbally adept.

4

Putting Learning Theory to Work

THE theoretical basis for the suggestions and techniques I've proposed is something you should understand. It's not that you have to become an expert about what goes on in your child's mind to implement the concepts in this book. It's just that once you realize what intelligence is as opposed to what schools proclaim it to be, you'll be motivated to try some new and different approaches. You may also feel more confident about trying these approaches if you're aware of how they fit with the universal way people (including children) learn.

I'm not going to present you with an esoteric, academic model. As much as possible, I'll illustrate points with child-centered examples and anecdotes so the discussion doesn't become disconnected from the subject at hand. Still, learning is learning. A middle-aged man's mind assimilates knowledge the same way a child's mind does. If you were to ask an octogenarian and an eight-year-old child to figure out how to use a computer, the mental learning process wouldn't vary in the slightest (though the speed at which each person learned might). Let's examine this process and how you can use it to your child's best advantage.

Experience, Reflect, and Fail

Learning occurs because of the following three "actions":

- **Having a wide variety of experiences.** There's a reason that the child who is involved in diverse activities learns more than a child who sits in front of the television five hours each day. As I've emphasized earlier, there's no substitute for actual and diverse experiences. *Doing* many different things is the starting point for learning. Your goal isn't to create a well-rounded child as much as one who is continuously entering into complex, unfamiliar situations. Over time, your kid will develop a treasure trove of past experiences to draw on when dealing with present situations. As we'll see, the memory of an experience helps us deal with a similar situation more effectively—or, to put a finer point on it, more intelligently.

- **Reflecting on these experiences.** From a learning standpoint, experience isn't worth much without reflection. This means not only thinking about something that happened but articulating this experience in the form of a story. Telling the story of an experience helps your child index the experience in her memory and makes it easier to retrieve at a future moment when she needs it. That's why you need to give children the alone time necessary for reflection and the one-on-one conversation time for them to tell you about all the weird and surprising things that have happened to them.

- **Experiencing failure.** You can't learn unless you're willing to fail. Failure provides the impetus to do something over and over again—to practice it—until you develop a certain expertise. For instance, kids who are afraid to get up in class and make an oral presentation will have difficulty developing their verbal ability. They don't take the risks necessary to accumulate the experiences that will help them become skilled speakers. As we have seen, expectation failure is the type of failure that is important from a learning standpoint. You expect one thing to happen and you're surprised when something else takes place. This unexpected result drives the learning process. When children's expectations are thwarted, they're motivated to ask, "What happened?" Ideally, they ask this question of themselves and explore a variety of reasons until they find an answer (though they can also seek help from someone else—usually a teacher or a parent).

Memory plays a crucial role in all three of these actions, though not exactly in the way you might think. Again, don't view learning as a trivia game where the winner has memorized the most facts. What I'm referring to here is the ability to summon just the right memory at just the right time.

The More Diverse the Experiences, the More Useful the Memories

According to one study, fish remember what they experience for about fifteen seconds. To some, this might seem like a good thing—fish will never get bored since their world is always fresh and new—but it also guarantees they'll never learn anything. In many ways, intelligence is memory. More specifically, it's having an accessible storehouse of experiences.

Children are much better than fish at remembering their experiences (though when you tell them to brush their teeth for the thousandth time, it may not seem like it). In fact, they're usually quite good at recalling the simple, obvious memory when they need it: Most kids remember how to make a sandwich when they're hungry, to do the edges first when they're working on a jigsaw puzzle, or any number of other practical things. Smarter kids, however, also summon useful memories in a more abstract and less linear way. When they're faced with a problem or a challenge, they think, "I know what to do here; I've had this experience before." This cognition isn't always conscious; it's sometimes described as intuition or instinct. But smarter kids' minds work this way all the time. Their memories supply them with a clever remark to impress a new friend (verbal proficiency), or they recall a story they were told a year ago that sheds light on how to put together a complex model airplane (analytical ability). In learning theory, this process is called reminding.

To understand reminding, think about how, during a conversation, you come up with things to say in response to things that are said to you. You have to be reminded about what you think about a given subject to express a thought about it. Our minds process everything we see and hear by comparison to what we've already experienced. Things don't just pop into our heads or out of our mouths in a random series of events.

Let's take the case of eleven-year-old Jerry, a Chicago boy who was on a hike in a nearby forest preserve with his friends when a fierce storm broke over them. As the thunder and lightning raged, Jerry's friends wanted to keep going because they thought it was fun to be out in the storm. The memory that entered Jerry's consciousness at that moment was of the winter vacation he had spent on his uncle's farm in Minnesota, and how his uncle had pointed out different animals' burrows as they were walking around the property. This memory led Jerry to analyze the situation as follows: If animals seek shelter in burrows during the fierce Minnesota winter, perhaps we should do the same during this storm. He convinced his friends to wait out the downpour under one of the shelters along the trail.

Why was Jerry reminded of this useful memory and his friends weren't? Because Jerry had had the unusual experience (for a city kid) of spending time on a rural farm. The current event and the memory of which we're reminded aren't always as clearly linked as in this example. Our mind indexes our memories in all sorts of abstract ways, and Jerry might have been reminded of the animal burrows on his uncle's farm only when his friend told a story of ice fishing in a shack (his mind could have indexed the story under the heading "unusual shelters" as opposed to "safety in a storm").

Nonetheless, the point is that the more diverse your child's memories, the more likely she is to be reminded of the right memory at the right time. When my daughter was six, she heard a Beatles song called "All You Need Is Love." I asked her if the song title was accurate; is love all you need? "No," she said, "you need power." At some point before this, Hana had been in a situation where she felt powerless; she really needed power and didn't possess it. Having had this experience, she was reminded of it by my question, and it prompted her to say something original and exhibit her creativity.

Or perhaps you recall the story about my daughter telling me that she would come back when she needed me again. The experience of my being available to help her in times of need is filed away in her mind. It's not filed in a specific, concrete manner—"when my blocks fall down, call Daddy"—but in an abstract way.

Myriad experiences alone are not enough to make people smarter. A good index-and-retrieval system must accompany these experiences, and this system is built on reflection and story-telling. If the experiences are sufficiently diverse and the child is provided with sufficient alone time, reflection will naturally take place. Storytelling is another matter, and one that parents can facilitate.

Shaping Memories Through the Stories We Tell

People are storytelling machines. From the time we're born, we begin to accumulate experiences and translate them into stories. I'm using the word "story" in the broadest possible sense. We tell short, cryptic stories, such as in the movie *Manhattan,* when Isaac replies to Mary's inquiry about why he got divorced: "My wife left me for another woman." We also tell much more involved, narrative stories with a traditional beginning, middle, and end.

Whatever form the story takes, the telling of it is crucial to learning. It's not a coincidence that the best storytellers are often the smartest, most successful teachers, salespeople, therapists, lawyers, and other professionals. The ability to tell stories in clear, compelling ways serves most adults well. In addition, telling a story forces us to think more clearly. If we tell someone about our trip to Egypt, we have to consider which details to empha-size and which events to omit. If we notice someone is falling asleep as we describe the construction of the pyramids in mind-numbing detail, we learn (I hope) not to use as much detail the next time.

But in terms of our discussion of learning theory, these aren't the reasons to encourage children to tell stories. From a learning standpoint, telling a story helps us remember and recall it better. Think about a favorite story, one you've told a number of times. Chances are you've probably embellished a few elements of the story to enhance its entertainment value. In fact, it may be diffi-cult for you to separate the embellishments from what really hap-pened.

Verbalizing stories facilitates the mind's labeling and retrieval process. If we don't articulate our stories, they float unlabeled in the nether regions of our brains and are difficult to retrieve at appropriate times. If we do articulate them, we can readily retrieve an old story that's relevant to a new situation. This ability to compare old and new stories is critical to intelligence. When we can do this, we're much better able to say something original or to analyze a problem more effectively. It allows us to be smarter in how we deal with situations.

Writing is another way to express these stories, and while this can be useful in the labeling and retrieval process, it isn't as effective as telling stories to another person. We need another person to challenge our stories or to validate them. When we say them out loud, we're looking for another person to respond affirmatively or negatively. Either way, that response facilitates the story's labeling. Penny is a twelve-year-old who has spent the past hour talking on the phone to her friend Mary. The subject of their conversation is Billy, a very cute boy in their class whom Penny thinks she likes and wants to ask to a dance. Penny, however, has reservations; she's seen Billy be mean to other kids, and he has a reputation for making fun of girls who like him. After Penny has gone on for a while about Billy, she asks Mary what Mary thinks of him.

"I think he's a jerk."

If Mary hadn't responded in this way, Penny's story about Billy probably would have remained ill-defined. Hearing Mary's clear and forceful response helped imprint this particular story in her mind. It confirmed her suspicion that Billy was indeed a jerk.

Parents need to encourage children to tell their stories and to reflect on them. As part of my research for an earlier book, I recorded the stories my children told when they were small. When Hana was three, here is what she told me happens when you go to a restaurant (her responses to my questions are in italics):

You go in restaurant, sit down, and eat food.
How do you get the food?
From the waitress.
How does the waitress know what to give you?
You ask for hamburger, she gives you hamburger.
What happens if you ask for hot dogs, do you get a
hamburger?
No, you get hot dogs.
What happens then?
You leave.
You leave just like that?
*No, the waitress gives you some money and you give some to
her and she gives some back to you and then you leave.*

A year later, Hana didn't need my questions to answer this
same question:

*You come in, sit at the table, the waitress comes and she gives
you a menu, then she takes it back and takes down your order,
then you eat what she brings, then you get up from the table,
pay the restaurant, and leave.*

In one year, Hana had learned how to tell a coherent story and
grasped certain concepts basic to a restaurant experience. During
the period between Hana's first and second story, I not only took
her to a number of restaurants, but I asked her to articulate her
experiences about them. I should also emphasize that she didn't
simply recite her experiences; we would discuss certain elements
of her story that confused or intrigued her, and I would give her
additional information about what a check and paying for food
involved. As a result of all this, the restaurant story and its related
concepts acquired a label that was easily retrieved by her mind.

It's never too early to encourage your children to tell stories.

It's a mistake to believe that a four-year-old child is incapable of telling a story or lacks a coherent story to tell. Our research shows that children are bursting with stories from the time they can talk. Unfortunately, some parents don't realize this because the stories aren't as "polished" as those told by adults. From the time Hana was three and a half, I asked her to tell me stories. Here is one I recorded:

> There was a little girl named Hanaranabana. She was riding her Hot Wheels and David was riding a car and they went up the driveway to the backyard and zoom, zoom they went . . . Papa took a walk with Hanaranabana and David and while she's riding she stopped at a stop sign and David said let's walk this way and Hana said let's walk that way and they turned. They were going on a real vacation and they turned and turned . . . and they got lots of presents, even a ruler . . .

What Hana did and what all children do when they tell these stories is make sense of their experiences. By talking about what took place in their lives—even when they embellish their stories or substitute what they wish would have happened for what really did happen—they acquire usable memories.

While children can tell their stories to others—friends, grandparents, teachers, siblings, therapists—they really need and want to tell them to parents. This fundamental need can be glimpsed years later, when a parent dies. The adult child feels profound sorrow for many reasons, not the least of which is that he'll no longer have that person to listen to his stories. There is no one better than a parent when it comes to listening to a child's story, to sharing the child's excitement and empathizing with the issues and feelings the story raises. When that child has an important story to tell—making a new friend, scoring a game-winning touchdown, receiving a job offer—his natural impulse is to call his parents and share the story. Allowing this impulse to flourish from the time a child can talk is one easy way parents can help kids learn and become smarter.

Telling Dream Stories

Dreams are another way to understand how the telling of stories fits into learning theory; they also provide parents with another tool to foster learning.

Let's begin with a truism: If we don't write our dreams down or talk about them shortly after they occur, we'll forget them. Once we articulate them in the form of a story, they tend to stick with us; they become labeled and are retrievable like any real experience. Just as relevant is the fact that when we turn our dream into a cogent story, we force coherence upon it. Most dreams are disjointed; they are like a poorly edited experimental film made by a drug-addled director. By turning this mishmash of events and feelings into a narrative, we improve our critical thinking process. So not only are we able to retrieve the dream, but we've interpreted it in order for it to make sense in the telling. What we remember is our more cogent version of what we dreamed.

But what's the point in remembering the dream? After all, it isn't real. The dream may not be real, but the expectations it deals with are. I'm not going to get into a Freudian analysis of why we dream; my concern here is simply with the role dreaming plays in learning. That role involves expectation validation. As part of the learning process, we seek explanations for unexpected or odd situations. If you've been going shopping at a certain store for years and then one day it has a closed sign in the window when you arrive, you begin testing explanations: Maybe it's now closed on Tuesdays; maybe it's always been closed on Tuesdays and I just never shopped here on that day; maybe the owner, who's rather old, decided to cut back on the hours he works. Expectation validation is largely an unconscious process. While you may consciously consider some of these explanations, you probably see the closed sign and don't give it much conscious thought beyond "I'll come back when the store is open."

Many times it's not possible to test explanations consciously (we're not aware of what our expectations really are, the issue is difficult to think about, etc.). Yet we naturally want to test some of the expectations we collected during the day. Thus, we test them in our dreams. The way our minds do this is to run "simulations" that often have little to do with reality. For instance, when my son was in eighth grade he dreamed that Keith Hernandez, then the first baseman for the New York Mets, enrolled in his school. In the dream, my son felt he should ask Keith—whom he idolized—to become editor in chief of the school newspaper. Keith accepted the job but allowed my son, who was the real editor in chief, to continue to be in charge.

As I talked about this dream with my son, we explored the realities connected to the dream. It turned out that my son wanted to encourage his best friend to work for the paper, but he was worried about what might happen to their friendship if he was his friend's boss.

The dream, therefore, was testing my son's expectations about dealing with someone he respected. He was concerned about how he expected his best friend might react to his offer of a job. In the dream, this situation was simplified. All the difficult emotional issues and complexities of dealing with a best friend were removed from the equation. The dream simplified the situation by substituting a sports hero for his best friend.

Now I'm not saying that the dream held the solution to my son's problem; just because Keith Hernandez was perfectly content to let my son run the paper in the dream doesn't mean that his best friend would be happy being bossed around by my son. The dream, however, allowed my son to test one aspect of his expectation. By talking about it, we could bring the issue closer to home and turn it into a memorable experience that might be useful later on.

For these reasons, I would suggest that when kids wake up in the morning, the best question you can ask them is:

Have any interesting dreams?

Young children love to talk about their nightmares as well as dreams that are just plain weird. These are exactly the dreams you want them to talk about. The more unusual or outrageous the dream, the more kids are compelled to seek explanations for them.

Encouraging Kids to Tell the Stories They Care About

You should understand that the idea isn't to get kids to tell any old story but the ones they care about. The stories that are really important to them revolve around: "Am I any good at this?" "Do other kids like me?" "Why can someone do X better than I can?" You know what your kid's interests are, the topics that turn him on. Even if these topics strike you as mundane or idiotic, these are what you need to encourage children to tell stories about. You're not going to have much luck if you ask a child to discuss what he learned in a hated math class.

My daughter once asked me who I would vote for if she and her brother were running against each other for president. This was the story of "Who do you love more?" and when my daughter was little, this was a very important story for her. When I told her that they probably would never run against each other, she changed her approach, wondering who I would root for if she played for Pittsburgh and Joshua played for Dallas. As she told these stories, Hana was trying to make sense of her experiences, to interpret her stories for herself. All this was important for her development. Being able to determine that I loved her and her brother equally helped her come to terms with the sibling rivalry issue. The next time something happened that made her think that I was favoring her brother over her, she had this story labeled and ready to retrieve.

Some children are reluctant to tell their stories. If this seems to be the case, prompt them. One of the easiest things parents can do is start the story for their children: "We went to the zoo and we saw _____." By encouraging them to fill in the blanks, you rev up their storytelling engine. Pretty soon, they'll be off and rolling on their own.

Finally, recognize that children—especially preteens—often don't understand or appreciate adult stories. Parents have a tendency to lecture like surrogate teachers, feeding kids facts that might be good for them but are as distasteful as spinach. If you're going to tell kids stories, you need to tell them stories they can relate to on their level. Stories that are dry and devoid of interesting elements won't stick; the child's mind will never find a labeled place for dull, fact-laden stories. What they might remember are stories that are filled with humor, outrageousness, and excitement that they can relate to.

Now let's turn to the third element of learning theory and the one that presents parents with their greatest challenge.

Learning and Failure Take Place Where It Feels Safe

Allowing children to fail is the hardest thing for parents to do. Putting the other two elements of learning theory into practice is relatively easy; exposing children to a diversity of experiences and encouraging them to tell stories about these experiences usually doesn't meet with much resistance. Failure, however, is anathema in our society. We are obsessed with success, and we are even more obsessed that our children succeed. Schools have turned F into a dirty letter, and everything kids do in school is geared toward avoiding failure.

Failure, however, drives learning. The experiences we must have and turn into stories aren't worth much unless they include failure. I'm not suggesting that kids will benefit from flunking all their subjects in school or being constantly rejected and rebuffed at every turn. Indeed, failing within a group—especially a group of peers in a school setting—is usually humiliating and doesn't foster learning.

Instead, what we need to do is prepare children for graceful failure. Contrary to what some people believe, failure isn't inherently debilitating. Small children fail happily; they'll fall down hundreds of time before they learn to walk. Parents must prepare their children to fail, and part of that preparation is simply putting them in situations where they're bound to mess up in some way. Consider this politically incorrect truism: Boys traditionally do better in our society than girls because they're more accustomed to failing. In the past, most boys were encouraged to play competitive sports and most girls weren't. As a result, many boys experienced failure time and again: striking out with the bases loaded, missing a key basket, having a pass intercepted.

While these public failures aren't the best kind because there is a degree of humiliation involved, they serve a purpose from a learning standpoint. They help kids overcome their fear of failure. Once you've experienced it a few times and survived, you realize that failing is not so bad, and you're willing to try something risky again. Eventually, you learn from your mistakes and succeed.

Our culture, however, sends a strong message to parents that it's wrong to "push" kids, to force them to do things that are risky in any way. "Don't push Joan to take piano lessons, she's not ready yet," the culture says. "If she finds it too difficult, her self-esteem will be hurt." Perhaps there is some emotional hurt attached to failing. But it's relatively short-lived and easily overcome if parents handle it appropriately. On the other hand, a child who is never pushed toward graceful failure is usually a child who is scared to death to try anything new. This child will be stuck with limited experiences, limited stories, and limited intelligence.

Parents need to create an environment where it's safe for a child to explore, try new things, and fail. Just as they plug up electrical outlets so small, inquisitive toddlers don't stick their fingers in them, parents must child-proof the emotional environment so that kids aren't harmed by their failures. This means pushing them to try things that may be a little frightening and not berating them if they don't do something properly. You want them to stretch themselves, but not to the point where they're attempting a task that's not age-appropriate. Asking a seven-year-old to read *Ulysses* would be counterproductive. The better you know your child, the easier it will be to know in which direction you should push him to fail. If your daughter is interested in reading, then that's where you push her to read challenging books.

But if she comes to you and complains that the book is too hard and that she can't understand all the words, don't accuse her of being lazy and unmotivated, come up with another choice.

When my son was four, I encouraged him to recite the traditional "four questions" in Hebrew during our Passover seder. My mother was aghast, protesting that he had no business trying to say them at his age. In fact, he did make a number of mistakes in his recitation. But I didn't accuse him of being a disgrace to his religion or criticize him in any other way. Instead, I helped him with the words he missed and along with everyone else at the seder dinner congratulated him on his effort. Today, my son is adept at speaking in front of groups and can recite the "four questions" like no one's business.

What Takes Place in Our Minds When We Fail

Earlier I noted that we need to fail in a very specific way in order to learn. Expectation failure is relatively easy to understand on the surface: We expect one thing to happen and are surprised or even shocked when something else takes place. We naturally want to know why things didn't go as expected and begin searching for an explanation. This process, when repeated enough, allows us to discover what went wrong and how we can make it right the next time. This is what learning is all about.

Beneath the surface of this process, however, a number of more complicated events are taking place in our minds, and they have to do with the nature of expectations. Our minds contain more expectations than you might imagine. Even as I write this sentence, you're forming an expectation about what word will be . . . *next*. We walk into a room in our house and expect the furniture to be arranged a certain way. When we meet a friend for lunch, we have certain expectations about how he'll look. If those expectations aren't met, we wonder about what's different. Did he just grow that mustache? Is he sick? Has he gone on a diet? We don't consciously list our expectations when we see this friend; they simply come to mind based on our previous experiences. When there is no expectation failure—when our friend looks exactly as he did all the times before—we don't seek explanations and we don't learn anything new.

The irony about expectations is that to acquire them, we have to abandon them. Our expectations are consistently wrong. Experiences demand that we modify or completely change previous expectations. If we are served a meal the first time we fly on an airplane, we expect to be served a meal every time we fly. When we are served a snack the second time, we have to modify our expectations. When we fly on a foreign airline the third time and the meal it serves is delicious, this comes as another big surprise. In reality, expectation modification can be a bit confusing.

It may be that we fly three times and we're served the same lousy meal on each flight; this reinforces our initial expectation. The fourth flight, however, doesn't serve a meal, so we're really surprised that what we thought would happen didn't come to pass. Though I know of no study on the subject, I suspect that many gambling addicts are created because they win the first few times they visit the casino or racetrack. They expect to win every time after these experiences and have trouble modifying their expectations when they start losing.

This is why multiple experiences are important. The more we experience something, the better we become at seeing the nuances attached to our expectations. With a diversity of experience, we don't become locked into one expectation. Children with a narrow range of experience cling to their expectations; they find it difficult to modify and abandon them. Some teenagers, when they go out to eat, expect to have a fast-food experience and won't tolerate deviation from this norm. More significantly, they expect all courses taught in school to be boring (not a totally unfounded expectation) and won't admit to themselves that they find a new course somewhat interesting. When children have difficulty abandoning their expectations, they avoid or flee from situations that might force them to do so. The result in this case might be dropping a class that they actually find interesting.

Seeking Explanations

Sometimes when children experience expectation failure, they are motivated to seek explanations for what happened on their own. Sometimes, however, expectation failure is a complicated experience that children aren't able to deal with all by themselves. They reflect on their failure and can't make heads or tails of why they failed. In the past, they did the same thing and everything went according to expectations. They're stymied and may not seek an explanation unless you help them.

Let's say your child is a violinist and has been first chair in the school orchestra violin section for the past two years, securing that position every few months by playing well during sectional tryouts. At the most recent sectional, she felt she played as well as she had in the past, but this time she wasn't chosen as first chair. She's mystified and unwilling to delve deeply into why this happened. Perhaps she's reluctant because it's too emotional an issue to address; she feels that she's let her orchestra teacher down and is worried that she'll break down if she tries to talk with her about it. Maybe the obstacle to seeking an explanation is her own conviction that she's the best violinist in the orchestra and that there's no reasonable explanation for her demotion.

You can help your daughter eliminate the obstacle between herself and an explanation by telling a story. Rather than directly confronting her with possible theories about why she was demoted, tell an "analogous" story. Talk about the time you weren't chosen to be captain of the chess team even though you were the best chess player or how you were passed over for a promotion at work even though you were the team's most productive member. Your objective is not to explain your daughter's failure for her. It's to give her another path to take in search of her own explanation. She may respond to your story about the chess team by saying, "It's not the same thing, Dad. Chess is all about winning and losing, and violin is about intonation and technique. I've always been better at both than Clarisse, and the only way she could have gotten better than me is if she practiced her brains out or hired a private teacher . . . I wonder if she has a private teacher?" Maybe she'll ask and find an explanation. In response to your story, she told a story, and by doing so may have shed some light on why her expectations failed and what she can do about it the next time.

Why Scripts Prevent Expectation Failure

Scripts are necessary for us to get through the day. As a set of expectations about what will happen next in a well-understood situation, scripts allow us to save time and energy when we do certain essential things. For instance, they allow us to go into a restaurant and order a meal without thinking; we don't have to reason out the hundred steps necessary to order a chicken salad sandwich. In a script such as this one, both you and the waitress know your well-rehearsed roles. With only minor variations, you and she will engage in the same dialog and series of actions as you've experienced countless times before. This restaurant script can be altered somewhat by experience—a new trend such as free refills on soft drinks is incorporated into the script, for instance—but certain basic elements remain the same. In one sense, these scripts are a substitute for thinking. Instead of having to infer, reason, draw conclusions, and invent novel behaviors to solve problems, we simply apply a script. It's a shortcut we take from thought to action. Especially as children, we're busy acquiring hundreds of scripts. The more scripts children and adults know, the more comfortable they feel about playing their roles effectively.

The conundrum, however, is that the more scripts you know, the less likely you'll be to experience expectation failure and put yourself in a position to learn new things.

Scripts promote rigid thinking. Actually, thinking really doesn't take place; it's more accurate to state that scripts promote unthinking reactions. Once we've memorized a script, we apply it with a sometimes ludicrous belief in its veracity. Think about your child's scripts. Does your child reflexively switch the car radio to *her* station no matter what type of music or news program you're listening to? Does he automatically make the same breakfast for himself day in and day out? Does she hang out with the same group of friends and avoid doing anything with kids from any other social group?

Children who are locked into scripts limit their learning opportunities; the more scripts, the less learning. They short-circuit the learning process from the start, decreasing the diversity of experience and by extension their chance of encountering expectation failure. Children gravitate to the unthinking comfort of scripts; it's uncomfortable for them to leave their jock friends at lunch and sit at the "geek" table. For adolescents, especially, it's tough to let go of scripts and encounter uncertainty and confusion. Even younger kids, however, cling to their routines and are nervous about trying something new (like eating ethnic food) or risky (venturing an original opinion in class).

The good news is that most inherently (i.e, genetically) bright kids are willing to break away from scripts. The restaurant test proves this point from an adult perspective. Ask a group of people whom you don't consider particularly smart where they'd like to go to lunch; the odds are they'll choose someplace safe, a restaurant they've all been to before or that serves standard American fare. Then ask a group of people whom you consider smart where they'd like to go to lunch. You'll probably find that they want to go to a restaurant they've never been to before that serves exotic or unusual food. Academics, who are generally pretty intelligent, are drawn to strange new restaurants; the weirder, the more out of the way, and the more adventurous the dining experience, the better.

Kids, much more than adults, naturally gravitate toward scripts; social norms cause them to want to watch television, eat at fast-food restaurants, and conform in many other ways. It's up to parents to force their children out of some of these scripts.

When and How to Push Kids Away from Scripts

It takes a certain amount of persistence to raise a smarter kid. By that I mean that your children may resist change and your attempts to move them away from the shopping mall script, the mindless chatter on the phone script, and other routines they gravitate toward. My son resisted change like crazy. When I told him I was sending him to day camp, he protested the idea, though once he was there, he loved it. When I told him he was going to overnight camp, he resisted leaving the first camp for a new one. Again, he eventually learned to love it.

If you give in to their resistance, you'll deny them the opportunity to fail at something new. As you'll recall from an earlier story, my son felt very lonely at camp at first; he failed at it in the sense that he expected things to be a certain way based on his previous camp experience and there were significant differences. He examined these differences on his own and with the help of a camp counselor (as well as the visit I made to camp), and he gradually learned how to go to this new camp. The experience turned out to be so rich and rewarding that for many years he returned to this camp as a counselor.

I'm not suggesting parents push kids away from scripts indiscriminately. If your child plays basketball all the time and is highly motivated to do so, that doesn't mean you should insist that he do football for a while, then tennis, then badminton. I'm all for kids practicing and mastering a subject they love. As you become increasingly more proficient in a given area—as you attempt more and more challenging activities in order to move up a level—you're bound to break out of the script and experience expectation failure. An anti-learning attitude exists, however, when a child refuses to move up a level—when she won't try out for the varsity team or refuses to attempt a more difficult piano piece. If your child really enjoys a particular activity, you need to keep pushing her to take risks with it, to try new and more difficult challenges within that area.

Trust your child's motivation. It's intrinsic to all kids; one will be motivated to fence, another to do science experiments, a third to build model airplanes. Once you discover what your child is motivated to do, you can push him toward expectation failure in that area. When he fails—when his science experiment doesn't turn out as he was sure it would—he'll be motivated to seek an explanation for the failure, to ask you a question, to look up something in a science book, to talk to his teacher at school.

Here's a more general though related piece of advice that jibes with this aspect of learning theory: Shake things up every now and then. You don't want your child to exist in a peaceful, Zen-like state. If children aren't placed in stressful situations occasionally, they won't have a chance to develop the six traits of smarter kids. You don't develop gumption if you never try sticking out an unpleasant situation. You don't develop verbal skills unless you get up in front of different groups of people and start ad libbing, debating, and telling stories. Most kids aren't risk-takers by nature. Given their druthers, they won't thrust themselves into places where they're not confident or feel uncomfortable. Certainly you don't want to put your children in situations where they're tremendously overmatched or where they're so terrified of what you're proposing that they'll be traumatized if they fail. But if the challenge is reasonable and you trust they can handle the stress, don't let their token resistance dissuade you from pushing.

Many parents tell me that they would never move to another part of the country for their work or even change schools because the move would "hurt" their kids. While children who like their neighborhoods and friends won't relish the prospect of moving, they will benefit intellectually from the change in environments. You're following the learning formula by forcing kids to experience new things. Inevitably, they'll be forced to take some risks if they want to make new friends (which most kids are strongly motivated to do), and they'll probably fail a few times before they get it right. But they'll have gained more experiences and stories than the kid who lived in the same place his whole life.

The Trade-offs

Failure produces angst in parents for a number of reasons, not the least of which is that it's tough to see your children under stress. When things don't go according to expectations, children react in all sorts of ways. Some become angry, others are hard on themselves, and still others are frustrated. You need to understand that raising a smarter kid involves trade-offs. If you protect your child against failure—if you allow him to stay within his scripts as much as possible—then you'll probably raise a child who has less stress in his life. By always living in the same place and never pushing him to try more challenging activities, you'll probably avoid a certain amount of child-parent tension.

Of course, you may also end up raising a child who has never discovered or developed an area of interest and has little chance for significant achievement.

Geniuses, innovators, and leaders generally have major personal issues with which they struggle throughout their lives. They're failing all the time, trying out new ideas that they were initially enthusiastic about and sure would pan out, only to find they were wrong. This is naturally upsetting. They are also constantly fighting norms and the status quo, floating plans and proposals that often meet with a great deal of resistance. Or they'll present what they feel is a great idea to a room full of people who react scornfully. Once again, their expectations have not been met, and it's not always easy to take.

Smarter kids have to endure some of the same feelings, albeit on a smaller scale. When a smart kid asks a provocative question in class or decides to write an essay that doesn't fall within the parameters outlined by the teacher, he's probably going to receive a negative response—mocking laughter from his peers and a bad mark from his teacher. When smart kids go beyond their scripts and take on new and challenging activities, they are bound to struggle for a while until they master the challenge.

Raising a smarter kid, therefore, isn't going to be smooth sailing. On the other hand, the failure doesn't have to be as devastating as it might be. Remember earlier examples of how toddlers are perfectly happy to fail at walking, eating, and other activities until they get them right?

Older children have the same innate capacity to rebound from failure, especially when their failure occurs in private. In working with organizations, we've found that people willingly take risks and fail when working on computer simulations of typical business problems. For instance, if they're asked to deal with a problem employee and they do so in a way that makes a bad situation worse, they don't feel like idiots. They're able to rebound from their expectation failures and try another approach because they haven't been subject to public humiliation. It's that public flogging that makes people steer clear of failure and stick to their scripts. School has institutionalized such floggings, at least of the verbal variety.

While you can't protect your child from these experiences in school, you can encourage self-exploratory learning that allows him to fail in private. Push him to tackle difficult projects outside school. Support him when he does become frustrated or upset over a failure. Make time for him when he has a question about the failure. Drop everything and listen as he explains what he expected to happen and his disappointment over what did. Point him in a direction (the Internet, the library, an expert in a given subject) that will help him figure out why he failed.

Your goal should not always be to take the sting out of failure; it should be to offer the kind of support that makes it all tolerable.

2

The Six Traits of Smarter Kids

5

How to Raise a More Verbal Kid

LET'S begin with a simple premise: The more verbal a child is, the more intelligent she seems. No matter what your child decides to do with her life, verbal ability will have an enormous impact on her degree of success. People who communicate clearly, respond quickly and cleverly, tell interesting stories, and make compelling arguments have a distinct advantage. Those who don't are put at a disadvantage; we assume that their halting speech and poorly phrased utterances are signs of stupidity.

I was visiting a friend one morning and her son was in the bedroom, flipping through the channels with a television remote. His mother introduced us, but as I tried to talk to him, he continued to flip through the channels and barely said a word. This is a child who is used to watching and listening, not to talking. He may be a brilliant boy, but I automatically assumed he was slow. This may not have been a fair assumption, but it's one most people would make based on his inability to respond with well-articulated words.

As a professor whose job it is to stand in judgment of students, I am always impressed by someone who is articulate. When I interview job candidates, I begin by saying, "Tell me about yourself." Some talk in a neutral tone about their job history, reciting facts without much passion or persuasiveness. Others are very clever and share strange but entertaining ideas about who they are and what they've done. And then there are those who look confused, shrug, and ask, "What do you want to know?" For me, the interview is usually over at that point.

It might be argued that some people—any number of politicians come to mind—are superior communicators yet don't have an original thought in their heads. It might be argued that their verbal ability is mere camouflage for a barren brain. It might also be argued that their way with words is a distinct form of intelligence; that this is what helps them be effective, successful people and overcome their genetic disadvantages.

Without delving too deeply into the semantics of the subject, let's assume that you have a reasonably bright child possessing a mind teeming with original thoughts. If, however, your child never learns how to express those thoughts, teachers, prospective employers, and bosses will assume him to be ordinary at best and dumb at worst. Verbal ability, therefore, is what people require to show their intelligence to the world.

Two Essential Speaking Skills

To help you understand the two verbal skills necessary for success in our society, let me tell you a story about linguistics. Holland and Germany are neighboring countries, but the Dutch and German languages are significantly different from each other. If you speak Dutch, you don't understand German, and vice versa. Typically, languages are different from one another because of geological or manmade barriers—mountain ranges, oceans, walls. In the case of Germany and Holland, however, there is no barrier besides a tiny river. Why, then, are their languages so different?

If you go to Utrecht, a town in western Holland, and walk east to the neighboring town, you'll find that there's a slightly different dialect spoken, but each town can understand the other's language perfectly. As you walk across Holland and through Germany, you'll discover that every town can understand the language spoken in the town immediately to the west and east. In fact, the easternmost town in Holland and the westernmost town in Germany can understand each other because their dialects are so similar. If, however, you arrive in Berlin (in far eastern Germany) and speak to people in Utrecht dialect, they won't have the faintest idea what you're saying.

Let's return to the question of why this is so by way of a linguist's joke: What's the difference between a language and a dialect? The answer: A language has an army. At some point in history, the Berlin part of Germany gained great power and conquered the lands stretching all the way to Utrecht in Holland. When it did so, it declared that everyone must learn to speak "official" German, which was the German dialect spoken in Berlin. For survival and economic purposes, most people learned the official language. Still, they also retained their particular dialect, speaking it among townsfolk and when Berlin natives were absent.

Children must learn to speak both their dialect and the official language to do well in life. They need their dialect so that they can communicate effectively in their community, and they need facility with the official language to succeed in the larger world. Go to Atlanta and listen to the newscasts; you rarely hear a television anchor with a southern accent. In academia, many distinguished professors grew up in New York, but very few speak with a pronounced New York accent. Speaking the right language is crucial to acceptance and success. If you're in advertising, you need to learn how to speak official advertising-ese. If you're in banking, you need to become proficient in speaking like a banker.

Unfortunately, many parents don't raise their children to speak the official language. If the parents speak in colloquialisms or sound uneducated, the odds are that their children will speak that way too. There's been a great deal of talk in recent years about "black English." Some of the critics of Ebonics and similar movements say people who use black slang are "speaking improperly." This is nonsense; they're speaking perfectly correctly according to the unwritten rules of black English. A problem arises when they don't also learn how to speak the language of mainstream society. If they don't learn this second language, they're viewed as less intelligent than those who do.

Learning a second language isn't always easy. I grew up speaking a Brooklyn dialect full of Yiddishisms. For years I thought "aggravation" was a Yiddish word and "klutz" was an English one. Even as an adult, I sometimes revert unconsciously to my dialect. I once was playing handball with a Venezuelan, and the environment caused me to talk as I did as a handball-playing kid in Brooklyn. The Venezuelan told me he couldn't understand my fractured English.

Assimilating your language to the norm of the group you want to belong to requires conscious effort. Ideally, parents will speak both in dialect and in the official language, and their kids will grow up naturally bilingual. If parents don't speak this official language, they should at least put their children in situations with people who do speak it. If children get enough chances to speak to eloquent adults from an early age onward, they'll speak fluently in both languages.

What to Do (and Not to Do) Right from the Beginning

If you want to raise a verbal kid, you should start having conversations with him from the time he's born. Just because babies can't talk doesn't mean they can't listen. Talking to children frequently, articulately, and from an early age is the simple trick to raising a verbal kid. In practice, it's a tough trick for many parents to perform. Let's look at some of the do's and don'ts to understand why this is so:

1. Don't let someone else raise your child.

Do you want your kid to talk like the person who works at the day care center or the au pair who speaks broken English? Children are great mimics, and their speech patterns and fluency will reflect those of the adult they're with most often. Consequently, the trend to place children in day care or with nannies or au pairs from the time they're six months old is a very bad trend. I realize that some people don't have a choice economically or that both husband and wife are dedicated to their careers, but parents should recognize that this practice often handicaps their child from a verbal standpoint.

Those first few years are crucial to a child's verbal development, and if you're not there to model the right type of speech, then you should carefully choose who is there. If you can find a nanny who speaks beautiful English, that's certainly better than one who speaks like Gomer Pyle. Of course, a nanny or other caregiver probably won't know about the other do's and don'ts or care enough to follow them.

2. Speak to your children as if they were intelligent human beings.

Parents who talk baby talk to their kids should have pacifiers stuck in their mouths. My cousin and I both have children the same age. When our children were three, she asked me why her child's speech was so far behind my daughter's. I asked her if I could observe their interaction for the next hour or so, and she agreed. What I observed was my cousin saying to her child in a singsong, high-pitched voice, "Want to ride the horsey now?" What a surprise that her child spoke baby talk!

When you're speaking to your child, use full rather than partial sentences, avoid baby words and silly intonations, and use your normal vocabulary rather than a highly restrictive one. Don't talk down to them. In fact, talk to them like little adults.

3. Don't criticize and lecture about their verbal mistakes; do make quick corrections.

When kids begin to learn how to talk, they make all sorts of grammatical mistakes. When this happens, don't constantly interrupt and say things like "It's not 'not go never'; that's a double negative and poor syntax." Don't make fun of the child's mistakes or be harshly critical. Even a patient, kind lecture about the proper way to speak versus the improper way is a bad idea. If you throw too much verbiage at a small child and if you do it in a way that's harsh or angry, he'll turn off whatever lesson you're trying to impart.

The alternative is to take advantage of a learning reflex all kids have. A child says, "I goed home." If you immediately respond, "I went home," the child will automatically repeat what you said. If you use an unfamiliar word when you're talking to him and it strikes his fancy, he'll immediately try using it in a sentence. This imitative reflex is built into every child's system, and you just need to be aware of how you speak to a child to trigger it in a productive way.

4. Extend children's thoughts.

Children need the opportunity to express their ideas about the things they're interested in and care about. Watch for opportunities to extend a child's thought. Let me give you an example of what I mean. My daughter often heard me tell her, "Enough chazarei," when she was little. "Chazarei" is a Yiddish expression for junk food (literally, it means pig food). One day she said, "Want chazarei!" To her, the word signified stuff she liked. Children don't always learn the real meanings of a word because they first grasp what the word means in context. I could have taught my daughter the proper sense of the word, but that's not really possible with a one-and-a-half-year-old child. What I chose to do instead was to watch my use of this word more carefully in the future.

What you can do in this situation—or at any opportune time—is extend the thought by using it as an opening for conversation. You can talk about what foods are chazarei, which particular one she wants, what she likes best, when would be a good time to eat such food, and so on. The issue is not just the obvious one of teaching the meaning of words, it is also about having a conversation in the first place. Children who converse cannot fail to become good at conversing.

At some point, every small child will say to a parent, "I want to play." Rather than saying fine, go play, give him the chance to elaborate. Ask questions such as "What do you want to play? Do you want to play outside? Why do you want to play that particular game?"

You can extend thoughts even when children haven't learned how to speak. Typically, toddlers will point to something they want, like a cookie, and make insistent sounds, and parents will give them what they want without saying anything. This is a missed opportunity to develop a child's language ability. What parents should do is ask, "What do you want? Do you want a cookie?" After this question is repeated on a number of occasions, the child will eventually say, "Yes, cookie." You've provided the child with strong motivation to extend his thoughts into words.

5. At times, separate your children when you talk to them.

This is something I wish I had done more of when raising my two children. Hana, as the older sibling, would often answer for her brother when I asked a question. When he started to talk, Hana would interrupt and say, "This is what he means." Older siblings often take the words right out of their younger siblings' mouths. They make it easy for them not to talk, and this is one reason that the youngest child in a family is usually the slowest to talk.

To counter this effect, spend more time alone with each child. This doesn't mean prohibiting them from playing together. But make sure you carve out time where you have conversations with each child independent of his siblings.

Talking and Intelligence Go Hand in Hand

As you help your young children develop their verbal abilities, you should understand that you're capitalizing on an innate response all children have to their experiences. I've had some parents tell me, "Well, my child is naturally quiet; he's very smart, but his way is to observe, listen, and reflect, not to talk a lot."

Certainly some children are genetically predisposed to talk more than others; my daughter babbled constantly before she learned how to form words and so she was probably "destined" to talk more than my son. So while I'm not disputing that some children are more talkative than others, I would dispute the notion of "naturally quiet." More accurately, some kids are quiet in public situations. When they're with adults, in school, or in any group setting, they become shy. But the vast majority of these children will talk up a storm in one-on-one situations with a parent or when they're with their best friend. This is true even with adults. A woman worked for me for three years, and I never observed her saying anything; other employees said she was the quietest person that they had ever seen. One day she was dropping something off at my Northwestern office, and I asked her if she would give me a ride home. During that time, she talked nonstop. Shy in public, she was outgoing in one-on-one situations.

Children, even more than adults, are bursting with ideas they want to articulate. Remember the three principles of learning: experience, reflection/articulation of experience, expectation failure based on experience. Kids have a greater need to talk about their experiences because they have many more new experiences than adults. When I was a child, my parents took me to the Coney Island zoo and made a recording of my voice. On the recording, they asked me what we saw at the zoo and I told them about the odd things the monkeys did. From a learning standpoint, what I was actually doing was articulating my experience based on expectation failure (I expected the monkey to stand around like a human being but instead he climbed on his cage and scratched himself in odd places).

I, like all children, had a tremendous need to share this expectation failure with my parents. It wasn't merely a social need but it was done to shape the memory of the experience. It's impossible for our memories to hold every detail of an experience. To create more room for important information, our minds reflexively erase details when we don't talk about them. When we tell stories about our experiences, however, we embed them in our memories. In effect, we're talking to ourselves as much as to another person.

Therefore, if you're going to raise a more verbal kid, recognize that this verbal ability comes with a learning bonus. The more children talk about their expectation failures, the more memories they'll have to learn from. If you listen to a child's story, you'll discover that it often begins with an expectation failure of some sort:

"Dad, I can't believe it, I got an A in math [when the child was expecting a C]."

"Mom, I have to tell you about this crazy thing Lydia did today [when the child didn't expect this behavior from Lydia]."

"Dad, I don't know what happened, I swung the bat just like you taught me, but somehow even though I swung level I missed the ball and struck out [when the child fully expected to get a hit]."

These expectation failures stick with kids; the next time they're in a similar situation, they're better prepared to solve a problem or continue a pattern of success. The boy who struck out will remember that last time the problem was that he didn't swing quickly enough; he'll remember this because he talked about what he did wrong and got some advice about what caused his expectation failure. In this way, the experience became part of his memory for later use.

Parents need to encourage their children to verbalize these expectation failures constantly. Not only will it make them more articulate, but it will help them shape their memories in highly intelligent ways, eliminating the trivial details and retaining the important ones (although it may not make them better baseball players).

Adolescence and School: Natural and Unnatural Obstacles to Speech

While schools might encourage students to raise their hands and "participate" in class, this has nothing to do with making them more verbal. Especially in middle school and high school, the classroom environment actually makes kids less verbal. Much of the problem stems from the fact that there are right and wrong answers, and few kids want to take the chance of saying the wrong one. When they do say something the teacher or fellow students deem wrong or "dumb" (often when they're called on even though they haven't raised their hands), they're humiliated. They never again want to speak in class.

Other kids do raise their hands and answer questions, but they often are doing so without any interest in what they're saying. Freedom of expression is severely limited in school. It's the rare teacher who doesn't set all sorts of boundaries about what can be discussed and how. Students are expected to give brief answers that supply accurate information. Even when they're asked to express their opinion on an issue, they must respond in an acceptable manner. This often means keeping their remarks brief, not drawing on personal experience, and avoiding humor, sidebars, spontaneity, or any of the natural elements of storytelling. They can't talk about what interests them; they must talk about what interests some curriculum head. Thus, their remarks are eminently forgettable, both by the class and by the speakers themselves.

The biggest problem, however, is that a child is only one of twenty-five or thirty kids in a class. It's difficult to achieve verbal expertise when you occupy such a small part of the stage. Children become more verbal when they engage in one-on-one conversation about something that interests them. Reading from detailed notes as you give a speech on a boring subject (and when you're scared to death) doesn't foster the type of verbal exchanges that make one more eloquent or even articulate.

You can undo the damage school does to your child's verbal ability by sitting down for family meals and talking. This is a pet peeve of mine—the lack of mealtime conversation between parents and children—and it's one that I'll return to later in the book. For now, let's look at it just from a verbal standpoint. Food and good conversation go well together, and this is a parent's opportunity to have children talk about ideas that interest them. This doesn't mean asking, "So, what did you do at school today?" Such a question often elicits responses such as "I don't know" and "Nothing." Instead, focus on a school-related subject you know your child is interested in. If he's on the basketball team and loves the sport, ask him about practice, the coach, and their next opponent. This will start a flow of stories about experiences and expectation failures related to these experiences ("I can't believe we lost to Lincoln, they have all these slow white guys." You might respond, "Why are white guys so slow?"). Parents can also talk about issues that are of interest to them and see if these issues trigger a child's interest. I have a friend who used to rant and rave at the dinner table about the trades the Mets made. Pretty soon, his daughter was asking questions and expressing her opinions about the trades. The subject interested her, she had the chance to express her ideas, and pretty soon she became positively eloquent about why you don't swap a pitcher for an outfielder even up.

As your kids get older and become adolescents, they naturally will become moody and quiet, especially when you ask them questions about issues that they feel are none of your business. As difficult as it might seem to talk to an adolescent, you still have many opportunities to help them develop their verbal skills. Here are some easy things every parent can do in this regard:

- **Take them on trips.** This is another technique that can enhance many if not all of our six traits. Here, the point is that if you take a child to see a farm when he's lived in a city all his life or go spelunking in a cave, he's going to talk about it. You don't have to take your children on extravagant trips to the far ends of the earth (though if you can afford it, such trips would be great). Just take them to places that interest them, whether it's the Rock and Roll Hall of Fame in

Cleveland, an archaeological site in your state, a wildlife sanctuary, or Civil War battlefields. If they're interested in the places you're taking them to, they'll start talking about them and asking you questions. If these are places they've never been before, they'll experience expectation failure and be eager to talk to you about these failures.

- **Tape them.** Audiotape is good but videotape is better. When teenagers see and hear themselves speaking, they are often surprised and dismayed at their inarticulateness. All those "likes," "ums," and repeated slang expressions embarrass most teenagers. What seems perfectly normal when they're with equally inarticulate friends becomes odd and disturbing when they see themselves in isolation. Though you don't want to use this too often or to make them feel bad about themselves, this technique is a good way to trigger expectation failure and get them to be more conscious about how they speak.

- **Make it your business to learn something about what they're interested in.** Whether it's a type of music, computer software, sports, or movies, take the time to know something about the subject. If you ask general questions about these subjects, your children will respond quickly and vaguely. If, however, you demonstrate some knowledge and share new information or ask informed questions, teenagers will be motivated to talk to you. It's also important to keep up with the knowledge level of your child. I've seen parents lose the ability to communicate as soon as their kids become more sophisticated about computers or music and the parents don't know enough to talk intelligently about the subject.

- **If they watch television, watch with them and make sure to talk about the program afterward.** As detrimental as television can be to verbal development, teenagers are drawn to it like moths to a flame. If you're going to allow them to watch a limited amount of television, use the program as a launching pad for a discussion or debate. News and news programs are terrific for this purpose, but you can probably generate a discussion out of any program that isn't a mindless sitcom or formulaic action show.

- **When you engage in conversations with your kids, push and challenge them.** You don't just want your kids to talk; you want them to talk convincingly. The ability to present and sell one's point of view to another person requires practice. Therefore, don't accept everything they say at face value. You don't want to put them down for their opinions or make fun of them, but you should question their assumptions and push them to rethink their ideas. All this not only helps them become better sellers of their ideas but keeps them talking.

Finally, I should emphasize that adolescents can develop their verbal skills in conversations with other adults, as long as it's a one-on-one relationship with someone who treats them with respect. Coaches, teachers, aunts and uncles, and others can all engage in productive conversations, especially if the adult has knowledge about an area that interests the teenager.

On the other hand, most conversations between teenagers hamper rather than enhance verbal competency. For one thing, teenagers tend to speak to one another using all sorts of juvenile slang that is unacceptable in the adult world and conveys stupidity rather than intelligence. Just as troubling is the anti–intellectual current that runs through teenage culture. Highly articulate, smart-sounding kids are even put down if their peers think they are "too snotty" or showing off. While teenage conversation is important for socialization purposes, it can work against developing verbal skills.

Ultimately, parents are in the best position to help their kids develop these skills at all ages. If you're a reasonably articulate adult, you can expect your child to match or even exceed your ability in this area as long as you take the time and make the effort to talk to him in the ways discussed here.

6

How to Raise a More Creative Kid

WHEN parents think about helping their children be more creative, they usually think in terms of the arts, encouraging their efforts at drawing, writing, dance. The refrigerator has become an art gallery where parents proudly display their children's renderings of sun, moon, and stars, insisting that an asymmetrical, surreal landscape means their child is a true artist. Some people funnel their children into Suzuki violin lessons, believing they are allowing their children to express their creativity through music.

While unstructured drawing is great for kids and developing musical ability is a wonderful thing, this is not what creativity is about. Unfortunately, society reinforces the notion that the arts are synonymous with creativity. As you'll see, creativity is not an elite talent but something that everyone exercises to one degree or another.

Let's Define Our Terms

Here is a simple way of getting at what I mean by creativity:

When you're being creative, you're doing the unexpected.

My daughter took a creativity test in kindergarten, and as part of that test she was presented with a circle and asked to turn it into a picture. She knew they wanted her to draw a "smiley face" or something similarly mundane; instead she turned the circle into a moose, and as a result of this unexpected drawing she scored off the charts in terms of creativity.

Children who learn to march to their own drummer, ignore the rules, and single-mindedly pursue their own "wacky" ideas are the ones who exhibit real creativity. This is the scientific model of the inventor, the Einstein or Edison who obsessively follows his own vision and experiments with it in ways that strike others as odd or even crazy. It's not surprising that many great scientists did poorly in school because they did not meet the expectations of their teachers or abide by classroom rules. A certain amount of craziness and anarchy comes with the territory. The kids who shout out answers in class, say weird things, and write papers on subjects that have little to do with the assigned topic are often the most creative.

It's also important to emphasize that we're all born creative, at least creative with a lowercase "c." That doesn't mean we all have the potential to become a great inventor, artist, or entrepreneur; it does mean that we all have the capacity to come up with and pursue our original ideas. Linguistics professors are astonished at the human capacity to create one original sentence after another. We may not be saying anything profound, but we are putting words together in ways we've never put them together before.

Rather than repeat the same sentences over and over, we invent new thoughts and invent ways of expressing those thoughts.

Creative people don't keep their unexpected thoughts to themselves. They express them, and they are often willing to do so in provocative ways. As adults, creative thinkers are willing to stand up in meetings, propose new ideas in new ways, and take the heat that such ideas generate. No matter what field your child chooses, this ability is crucial. Recently there was a merger between two oil companies. It came about because someone from one of those companies rose at a meeting and proposed the merger. This may not seem like a brilliantly inventive idea. In fact, it's not brilliantly creative with an uppercase "C." But by my definition it is creative. No one expected him to suggest this merger. People in the meeting probably criticized the concept and told him it was nuts. To make the merger happen, he had to stick to his guns and keep bringing up the idea, refining it in highly original ways.

Many people reflexively shoot down original and unusual ideas. Notice the next time someone proposes an odd or precedent-setting concept. Usually a smile or even laughter will accompany the articulation of the idea. The smile and laughter are defensive reactions to expected derision; the proposer is protecting himself from the scorn and snide remarks that experience tells him original concepts produce. The smile and laughter are ways of saying, "See, I'm not really that serious about what I'm suggesting." This defensive mechanism develops at an early age; kids do this in school all the time. If they're clobbered enough, they'll simply stop voicing their original notions.

As a parent, you need to develop a creative attitude in your children and recognize that school will attempt to squelch this attitude from kindergarten to college.

The School's Limited View of Creativity and What You Can Do About It

School encourages creativity within very specific norms and structures, and few worthwhile things have been invented within norms and structures. The Wright Brothers invented the airplane because they were willing to fly off a cliff hundreds of times. Edison invented the lightbulb because he played around with all those different filaments. The truly creative person has an insane devotion to an idea, banging away at it from all sorts of angles in all sorts of ways.

School doesn't permit this. It would say to the Wright Brothers, "You can't leave the school grounds and find a cliff to fly off." It would say to Edison, "We have only two hours to spend on filaments; it's time to move on."

Teaching to the test, the inflexibility of curriculums and policies, and the mass production of students stifles creativity. This is the nature of school; certain material has to be covered and certain tests have to be passed. The idea of a child obsessively working on one project for the entire year is antithetical to the school experience. Teachers generally don't tolerate students who go off on tangents or say unusual things. Personally, they may want to tolerate these things and recognize their value, but they're under pressure to have their students learn the facts, get through the syllabus, and score well on the tests.

You see this attitude even in graduate school, where students are supposed to write an "original" thesis. In reality, it's only original within very narrow boundaries. Students often just tweak a topic a bit; they apply standard methodology and come up with a variation on a theme. When I wrote my thesis, I was shot down because it was about having computers understand English. I was fascinated by the process of creating mental representations of sentences and trying to get computers to recognize them. My professors asked: What does this have to do with linguistics; what does this have to do with psychology; what does this have to do with computer science? In truth, it didn't have much to do with any of these subjects. As a result, no one knew what to make of my thesis. It was odd; it violated their expectations; it was creative.

But few saw it from that perspective. When teachers are unable to categorize something, they tend to view it as bizarre rather than innovative or original. Not only teachers but most people find it difficult to respond to creativity that goes far beyond their norms. They can appreciate an idea that's a bit more creative than what they're used to, but they have trouble grasping creativity that is more than one step removed from where they are. A teacher may appreciate a student's moderately creative theory about Hamlet's tragic flaw, but this same teacher probably would not find anything creative (no matter how well-conceived) about why Shakespearean language no longer possesses the power and poetry it once held for earlier generations.

The point of all this is that school will not encourage your child to develop his natural creativity. To help you take on this role, I'll provide you with ten maxims that will guide your efforts in this regard. First, however, let me suggest a few simple things every parent can do to foster creativity in a child:

- **Take your child's wacky ideas seriously.** When your child tells you that he believes he has psychic powers or that the moon is made of green cheese, don't tell him he's wrong or is being ridiculous; don't laugh at him or criticize him. Instead, ask him questions and discuss the idea with him. Give him the chance to take the idea in another direction or to discover himself that it's wrong. When I have an idea, I sometimes say to the individual or group to which I'm presenting it, "Here's a new idea, but none of you gets to criticize it." Ideas are delicate things, and they need room to grow. As easy as it is to shut down the creative impulse in adults, it's even easier in children.

- **Play with your child's ideas.** It's astonishing to me that parents who are perfectly willing to play catch with their child are unwilling to toss ideas back and forth. A few years ago, I helped produce a software program called Swale, designed to make computers creative. Swale was a top race-horse who died. To build the program our research involved asking students to find explanations for why he died. Typically, the students tried to use existing standard explanations: "He died of old age" or "He was killed for the insurance money." By feeding them a bit more information and bringing in ideas from other domains, we could motivate the students to become more adventurous with their explanations. For instance, the deaths of Jimi Hendrix and Janis Joplin may seem unrelated to the death of Swale, but when we proposed this idea, students came up with a string of relevant explanations. Both rock singers died from an overdose of drugs, and while the students certainly understood that the horse didn't take drugs on his own or harbor suicidal impulses, the discussion of drugs led to the notion that perhaps the horse was given drugs to help him win races; it suggested that he might have been killed because gamblers who had given the horse the drugs were afraid of being found out.

    Instead of giving your child explanations, encourage her to find her own. This is a natural impulse; children always want to know things like what happens after you die or how do birds fly. Give them some information, "what ifs," and encouragement, and they'll surprise you with highly creative explanations.

- **Encourage creative play, especially in younger children.** Have your child do things by herself that lack rules or structure. Playing with dolls is a terrific activity for children. So is any "made-up" fantasy game in which a child sits and invents characters, songs, and scenarios, using toys or anything else as props. Nurturing creativity in children means giving them time to play alone and without a strict set of rules rather than pushing them into a full program of regimented activities. Lessons and play groups should not dominate a child's free time. While some of this is okay, it should be balanced with time for creative play.

Maxims to Create By

In many ways, the struggle to raise a creative child is a social issue. If you implement the following ten maxims, you may find that your child is acting in ways that seem unconventional and even antisocial. Creativity, as they say, comes with a price, and that price sometimes involves being perceived as "abnormal." This doesn't mean a creative child has to be a geek. But it may mean that a kid is eccentric or obsessive about a certain area of interest. The question that your child will always be asking himself in his attempts to be creative is: "How much mockery, criticism, and failure can I tolerate?" It's the same question all creative adults ask.

Many kids are surprising in just how much they can take in order to be more creative. Being original and inventive is satisfying in and of itself, and it's a naturally motivating goal for many children. Perhaps more important from a parent's perspective, creativity is a tool for success in many different careers. The ability to think out of the box and to be innovative is not just an attribute for scientists and artists; it has become crucial for businesspeople, teachers, lawyers, and many other professionals.

Developing a creative attitude in your child can be achieved through the general techniques I've suggested in the previous section. But it's important for you to understand not only the more specific things you can do in this regard but the context in which you can do them. Here is a unique ten-step process that can guide your efforts to raise a more creative child:

1. Train kids to look for anomalies.

If you're going to be creative, you need something to be creative about. Anomalies trigger creativity by focusing the mind on a specific problem and the need for a solution or explanation. Anomalies violate our understanding of the world as we know it, and since children understand relatively little about how the world works, their worlds overflow with anomalies. Anomalies are joined at the hip with expectation failure. When I rode my bike in Florida and saw garbage strewn all around that pristine setting, that was an anomalous event. I expected the usual clean path and saw the unexpected. This event got me thinking and I arrived at the original (though not startlingly original) explanation that the previous night's storm had caused the nearby lake to overflow and dump its detritus on the path. Similarly, in Ireland I noticed that most of the signs were in Irish though the ones advertising items for sale were in English. The anomaly raised questions, leading me to wonder what was going on and causing me to find an explanation (Irish nationalism dictates Irish signs, but merchants know that they'll have a better chance if the signs are in English).

When your children are small, point out anomalies to them. Say things like "I don't understand this" and "This doesn't make any sense." When they're a bit older, ask them questions about anomalous events or circumstances: "Why do you think everyone on our block except the Shapiros has a Christmas tree?" A sense of wonder is important to develop in kids (wonder in the sense of curiosity and contemplation, not just stupefied awe), and being aware of anomalies starts them wondering about the world around them.

2. Get your kids to listen.

Most of us think of creative people as expressing themselves rather than listening to others. They are driven to articulate their ideas and lack the time or inclination to hear others articulate theirs. Again, this misconception goes back to the artistic definition of creative. In reality, to be creative you need to listen in order to hear anomalies. People say anomalous things all the time, and if you're not paying close attention, you'll miss them. This is really a deep type of listening, in the sense that you're trying to come up with an explanation for the anomalous thing someone said: "Why did Joey tell me that he ate a hot dog when I know that he's a vegetarian?" In addition, this type of listening provides invaluable stories, events, attitudes, and patterns that good listeners can use to come up with an original explanation for an anomaly, not just today but weeks, months, or even years from now. As the next step indicates, creative minds need data.

Are you always telling your kids to listen, and do they ignore you? Then try modeling this listening behavior. When they tell you something, respond to the anomaly they've raised. It may be an unusual problem at school or difficulty with a once-close friend. Confront your child with his anomaly, with the unusual and complex events in his life. Kids are great imitators at an early age, and if they see you doing this, they'll end up doing it themselves. You might also turn anomalies into a game of sorts. When you're talking to your child, say something that is clearly and even outrageously anomalous: "I was walking down the street the other day and had just picked up a sweet roll when a three-headed lizard walked by. Then I went on to the cleaner's . . ." Give kids the chance to stop you and say, wait a second, what did you say? Once they get the hang of picking up on bizarre anomalies, they will focus on ones that are a normal part of everyday conversation.

3. Facilitate gathering data to support their explanations.

Encourage your children to look at the world around them before locking into an explanation. You want to raise your kids to have a healthy skepticism about explanations. This skepticism will prompt them to gather more information to test their ideas, anchoring their creativity in reality rather than whim. Groups of related anomalies are better than single anomalies; they provide greater motivation for kids to find explanations and increase the likelihood that these explanations will be valid.

This isn't a complicated step for parents to take. It's just a question of going back to our learning model and remembering the importance of having lots of experiences with your child and then talking about them. After you have these experiences, make generalizations about them. Talk to your son or daughter about what you've observed and involve them in making general statements based on these observations. For instance, you take your child to the zoo on a beautiful summer day and you notice that half the animals aren't in their outdoor cages, preferring to stay indoors. You recall that when you went to the zoo earlier in the fall, the same thing happened, only that different animals were inside and out. Then perhaps you look at the signs in front of the cages and point out the variations in thickness of fur, the native countries of different animals, and so on. Pretty soon, kids will put two and two together or at least make the effort to solve the puzzle. Generalizations are synonymous with explanations, and all kids can make them given sufficient data. With sufficient data, kids can come up with amazingly creative guesses, assumptions, and inferences.

4. Help them classify and invent new classifications.

Kids see a dog for the first time, learn the name of this creature, and create the classification of "dog." Children get bitten by a pit bull and invent a new category: "type of dog to stay away from." Behind each category is an explanation that defines and suggests the importance of that category. When our expectations about a category fail—we meet a pit bull that is affectionate—then we have to create a new category.

As a parent, you want to help your children create and abandon categories with ease. Essentially, what you're doing is helping them develop the trait of every original thinker: resilience in the face of rejection (either by others or by the facts).

Classifying is just another way of talking about generalizations, and you should be aware that generalizations are frowned on by society. It's politically incorrect to say that "blacks are better basketball players than whites" or that "men are faster decision-makers than women." But it is generalizations of this type that are the backbone of how we learn and of originality. The process goes like this: We make a generalization, see an anomaly that challenges the truth of that generalization, and are forced to come up with explanations for the anomaly. Eventually, this process leads to a new generalization/explanation that is often more accurate than the previous one. This is a highly generative process, and it allows us to be very inventive with the way in which we explain the world.

It's an unconscious process, but the goal is to make it conscious. By doing so, we can come up with interesting questions and original conclusions. Let's say that Mary is a fifth-grader who generalizes that the clique of popular girls at her school are all rich; she knows that some of them live in big, beautiful homes and they all have the coolest clothes. But then Mary happens to see where Jennifer, one of the popular-group kids, actually lives, and it's a hovel. Mary then has to ask herself (or others) some questions: Is Jennifer the only one in the popular crowd who is not rich? Is it possible that Jennifer is indeed rich but that rich people can live in unattractive homes? Perhaps Jennifer's family used to be rich but encountered a sudden misfortune? If this last question is true, does this mean that Jennifer will be dropped from the popular group? Answers to these questions may cause Mary to form the generalization that just because someone is popular doesn't necessarily mean that she is rich.

Don't be swayed by society's bias against generalizations and categories. Communicate that any type of generalization and categorization is welcome, even wacky ones. "Fat people always laugh a lot," kids might conclude, or they might decide that they hate everything that's yellow or that starts with the letter P. Don't dismiss or mock these categories, even if they seem absurd. Make it fun to come up with these groupings and the explanations behind them. You should also play with their generalizations so they're accustomed to changing them as events and situations dictate.

5. Encourage hasty generalizations.

Again, society doesn't advocate jumping to conclusions. Children who utter wildly improbable theories will be told by teachers to "think before you speak." I'm suggesting that kids should speak before they think. When kids articulate their odd and controversial generalizations, they are inevitably challenged by others. You want your child's generalizations to be put to the test. This will force him to defend, rethink, and reformulate many of his generalizations, resulting in even more original thinking. The first generalization may be neither right nor particularly original, but the second or third ones might be. If you don't verbalize your generalization, no one is going to push you to reach that point.

Therefore, create an environment at the dinner table or elsewhere that makes your child comfortable saying all the wild and unusual things on her mind.

6. Get your kids in the habit of explaining themselves and their world.

The type of creativity that interests me emerges in the form of theories, and explanations are best described as mini-theories.

Children, however, are often prevented from formulating original explanations. School, with its emphasis on following scripts and avoiding mistakes, doesn't give its brightest kids the chance to fail (or to fail very often or interestingly). Parents, instead of allowing their children to flounder about in confusion, tell them, "Here's what you did wrong; here's the right answer." In both cases, children aren't motivated to seek or craft explanations.

Here's a cautionary tale in this regard. John and Joyce's nine-year-old son, Tommy, has never spoken. One day at breakfast Tommy pushes away the new cereal his mom has put in his bowl and says, "This cereal tastes lousy." Joyce is tremendously excited and shouts for her husband to join them; they both can't believe their son has spoken his first words. "I can't believe it, you talked," his mom says. "We thought you were mute. Why haven't you said anything all these years?"

"Because until you gave me that lousy cereal, everything was fine."

You have to place your children in situations where things can and will go wrong. Don't be tempted to protect them; you're only protecting them from being the bright, creative kids they will become if they are challenged. Put them in situations where they're a bit over their heads; don't rescue them with your explanations. Their minds will naturally form explanations, and this is a highly creative act that you want them to practice as much as possible.

7. Give your child permission to ignore the rules.

When people always follow the rules, nothing interesting happens to them. We come up with original ideas as a result of being in new and unfamiliar situations; we need to have a diverse group of experiences in order to think about things differently. The broad base of experiences that is the basis for learning is especially important for helping children become more creative.

This doesn't mean you have to create a rebel without a cause. I'm not advocating encouraging your child to violate every social rule or ignore everything his teachers tell him to do. Most children, however, are not rule-breakers. They learn the rules from a very young age, encouraged by parents to "do what you're told." They know exactly how the school game is played, for instance, and they adapt their behavior accordingly. As I've mentioned, my daughter decided to ignore the "writing rules" when she was in school, choosing a style and subjects that she knew would not earn her top grades. As a result, however, she had far more diverse writing experiences than the other kids; she didn't have to stay within the limited range of acceptable styles and subjects.

Let me use myself as an example of this maxim. When I see a chance to ignore the rules and do something differently, I seize it. Once when I was traveling to Chicago from Milan, security was asking me a series of hostile and ridiculous questions. For example, they noticed an Israeli stamp in my passport and were quite obnoxious with the questions that followed. According to the rules, I should have dutifully answered all their questions objectively and concisely. Instead, I made trouble. I joked about their questions and answered some of them facetiously. They called in their supervisor, and I asked him if I looked like a terrorist. As it turns out, I actually did fit the profile of a terrorist, in that I had made a certain change in travel plans that conformed to the profile. I had an enlightening conversation with the airport supervisor about terrorism and learned a great deal that I would never have known if I had played by the rules. And the airline had to seat me in first class because it had given away my seat when I was delayed.

I'm routinely asked to lecture on subjects as diverse as ship safety and Spanish cinema, and this has to do with my ignoring the rules. Though I'm no expert in either of these areas, people know I'll have interesting (or creative) things to say about them. I have a backlog of experiences that helps me view most subjects from a fresh perspective; I've gotten myself into so many different types of situations that I don't look at an issue the same way as someone who has had a much narrower range of experiences because he's adhered to a given set of rules.

What I'm suggesting you do is make it acceptable for your child to break rules on occasion. He should be able to miss school to attend an event in which he's interested. He should pursue "adventures" that may require him to get in trouble at school or cause him to be viewed as odd or unsociable by others. Make it clear to your child that rule-breaking is not a sin in your family; that you're not going to punish him for thinking independently or exploring the world around him. This is easier to write than to do because your child will invariably do something of which you disapprove. As long as he isn't endangering himself or others, however, you need to swallow your disapproval and let him ignore traditional limits and rules.

8. Raise your child to distrust old explanations and ask why.

You're not going to be an original thinker if you accept standard explanations. Children who accept every authority figure's version of events—teachers, parents, older siblings, and so on—never learn to develop their own point of view. Remember, I suggested that creativity was doing the unexpected; these children always do what is expected because they accept everything they see and hear.

Many old, creaky explanations are thrust upon children. They are told they have to go to bed at a certain time because they need their sleep; that they must get good grades if they're going to be successful in life; that if they don't have anything nice to say, they should say nothing at all.

Raising your child to challenge these standard explanations won't make your life any easier; kids who ask why all the time can be a pain. But a child who asks why is going to find herself exploring all sorts of ideas; she's going to develop a broader understanding of the world and an ability to create her own explanations. To help your child develop this ability, don't raise her to believe that you or any authority figure has the only explanation. Encourage her to question what others tell her and search for her own understanding of why things happen.

9. Give your child room to let her mind wander.

Kids who stare out windows in school or who daydream when they should be doing their homework are castigated. They are thought to be slackers and victims of attention deficit disorders. In reality, they are the ones who are learning to be creative. We're often at our creative best when we're paying the least attention.

I reserve a specific time and place to let my mind wander. When I retreat to Florida in the winter, I sit on a porch that overlooks palm trees and water, smoke a cigar, and allow my mind to drift with the smoke. During this time, my nonconscious mind surfaces all sort of issues and problems and often presents me with avenues to pursue solutions. The same thing happens in a dream, where our nonconscious mind is highly creative in the images and ideas it crafts. The philosopher Wittgenstein said, "All creative thought takes place in three B's: bed, bus, and bath." In other words, it takes place when our minds are not focused on an activity, when they're not consciously driving toward a particular goal.

Here are two things you can do that will encourage a child to let his mind wander. First, try this experiment that I conduct with my graduate students. Place a pop bottle in front of your child in a room without distractions (TV, radio, books, etc.) and tell him you'll be back in a few minutes. When you return, ask him to write down exactly what he's thinking at that moment. Then have him trace that thought all the way back to the pop bottle. What he'll find is that his "idle" mind created a fascinating thread of ideas from the moment you left him looking at the pop bottle to the moment you returned. It will demonstrate that there is tremendous creative power in letting his mind wander, and it will encourage him to do it more often.

Second, give small children something "mindless" they can do that will give them the chance to let their minds wander. You can't simply tell a five-year-old, "Sit down, do nothing, meditate, reflect, contemplate." But you can give her a simple task, such as playing with blocks or cutting pieces of paper, that requires almost no thought. In effect, these simple activities function as my cigar and Florida porch do for me; they allow us to be alone with our thoughts.

10. Put your child in situations where he can fail without harm.

This learning mantra is especially relevant for raising a creative child. Think about what happens when expectations fail: You become confused, you grapple with your lack of understanding, and you search for an explanation. At some point early in his life, Picasso probably didn't understand why everyone was painting such boring pictures; it's likely he expected other painters to be more adventurous and was confused as to why they all conformed to the same or similar approaches. He searched for an explanation and decided it was because people are ruled by dominant trends in the art world, and that maybe it was worthwhile to try something new. No doubt, his first cubist painting met with some criticism for being bizarre rather than creative. Perhaps he explained the failure by deciding that the public wasn't ready for his innovations. Or maybe he explained it by concluding that he should become even more daring in his style to catch people's attention, and he began pushing the boundaries even further.

Treat your child like a little Picasso. Put him in situations where he has to search for explanations as to why he failed. You can do this even with small children. Building blocks are wonderful for this purpose. Kids pile them up until—surprise, surprise—they tumble down. This failure prompts children to wonder: Why did it fall? Did I build it too tall? Was my base not wide enough? What would happen if I had more blocks on the bottom to start out with and made sure everything was perfectly even? Interestingly, old-fashioned blocks are better for this than the newer Legos, in that the visceral tumble of blocks has much more of an impact on a child's explanation-seeking sense than a Lego construction that simply looks weird. Failure in a video game, too, has relatively little impact; it's an abstract form of failure that doesn't catalyze much thought.

What you want to look for are activities that your child finds interesting. Then you want to push her to experiment in the areas she finds challenging. When she messes up, you want to be there providing support and information so she feels comfortable trying again.

When your child becomes unafraid of failure—when she's willing to shrug off defeat or mistakes and try a new approach—that's when she's going to come up with an idea that no one else has had before.

7

How to Raise a More Analytical Kid

HERE are two examples of analysis paralysis. The first involves a new Florida law that mandates schoolchildren listen to thirty minutes of classical music daily, based on studies that show a correlation between improved cognition and listening to this type of music. The Florida lawmakers no doubt analyzed the relevant studies and came to the conclusion that if schoolchildren were force-fed Mozart on a regular basis, they would suddenly become brighter. Perhaps they assumed that the urban poor in their districts who were scoring far below the national average on standardized tests would dramatically increase their scores with the help of Mozartized brains. Motivated by dreams of being hailed as education pioneers and being reelected, these legislators seem to have jumped to certain conclusions.

Their leaps of logic are astonishing. For instance, do they really believe that listening to music will make someone a better writer? Or that hearing classical music will enhance the scientific reasoning ability of a child? Given the chaotic, self-destructive lives of many classical music composers, a case could be made that such music didn't help them become particularly clear-headed thinkers. While it may be true that the orderly, organized music of Mozart facilitates orderly, organized thoughts in some test subjects, there's no evidence to indicate that this benefit will translate to a broader base of children. The legislators have failed to ask all the questions good analysis requires:

Might quiet contemplation have the same positive effect on kids as music?

Might the results of these studies be difficult to translate to a wide range of students with a wide range of interests?

Might classical music distract as many children as it stimulates?

Might certain types of kids derive more cognitive benefits from jazz, from rock and roll, from New Age music?

Might classical music have the same impact on kids as it does on a number of concertgoers (inducing a soporific state)?

The other example—alluded to in the previous chapter—also took place in Florida. It involved a bike ride a companion and I took around a lake. As we rode along, we both noticed all sorts of garbage strewn about. Neither of us had ever noticed this sort of thing in the past, and the path had been clean only a few days before. My companion could not figure out where all this junk had come from. The explanation, however, was actually quite simple. There had been a torrential downpour the night before. The lake must have overflowed its banks during the storm and deposited the detritus from its bottom on the adjacent path.

This conclusion didn't require brilliant analysis. As bright as my companion was, however, she couldn't make the simple deduction based on the facts available.

Many kids are being raised with the same lack of analytical skills. Before looking at what you can do about this situation, let's define what analysis is and what many people—especially young people—are substituting for it.

Overrelying on Feelings, Intuition, and Blind Faith

At its most basic level, analysis is about drawing logical conclusions after examining the data. This process involves asking questions, creating hypotheses, reasoning out complicated issues, and making deductions and inferences. Analysis is important no matter what a child grows up to be; businesspeople need to analyze markets, scientists need to analyze lab experiments, and lawyers need to analyze cases.

Yet we often make decisions based on flawed reasoning or we don't reason at all. Think about how kids decide where to go to college. They often choose schools because they feel "comfortable" during their visits, because the campus is pretty, or because the people they meet seem nice. When I took my daughter to schools, she rejected one of them because she didn't like the way the other kids looked. Logically, you should choose a college because it offers the courses you want to take and has strengths in your areas of interest. Illogically, we rely on how we "feel" about things. I'm not discounting the importance of feelings when it comes to relationships. Feelings may also have a basis in fact and can serve as a good guide to decision-making. But to rely on feelings exclusively without factoring in analysis is nonsensical. If your feelings are based only on what you wish were true—or if you're too lazy to do the work analysis requires—then you'll probably make the wrong decision.

I often have arguments with people about religion in which I'll question how they know that their good works will be rewarded with a place in heaven or how they can believe in a merciful God given all the cruelty in the world. "I take it on faith," they respond. But what's the basis for this faith? Unquestioning acceptance is the antithesis of analysis. "You're being so rational," these religious people tell me. Of course. That's the point.

Many children grow up lacking analytical skills because of a combination of laziness and the failures of the educational system. In terms of the former, analysis is hard work. The impulse to question, hypothesize, and deduce needs to be nurtured, and when it's not, kids fall into bad thinking habits. Parents can foster lazy minds by providing pat "because that's the way it is" kinds of answers. The schools, however, have long been thought to teach analysis. After all, don't children learn how to reason through mathematical problem-solving? In reality, math reasoning isn't transferable to life reasoning. Figuring out how to prove a theorem doesn't translate into how to prove a point in a debate about capital punishment. Whenever people suggest to me that math teaches reasoning skills, I always ask them if they've ever met a mathematician. Mathematicians are not typically the paragon of the rationally lived life.

Other school subjects, too, provide little opportunity to practice analysis. When kids aren't being taught to memorize facts and regurgitate them, they're required to express how they feel about a given subject. When they are asked to analyze the causes of a war or the theme of a Shakespeare play, the analysis is an empty exercise if they don't possess the slightest interest in the subject they're analyzing. Science, of course, is all about analysis in real life, but in school it focuses on memorizing formulas and following procedures. If teachers gave kids the chance to experiment and form their own hypotheses in an area that intrigues them, they might derive some analytical skills from these classes.

With Scripts in Mind, We Accept Everything and Question Nothing

A script is nothing more than a natural assumption about a future chain of events. In other words, if A happens, we automatically assume that B, C, and D will follow. Scripts are inherent expectations about sequences in our lives. We all have these scripts in our heads, and they start "playing" in our minds as soon as familiar Event A occurs. We don't have to consciously think about what's going to happen when we enter our cars to drive because the car driving script is so familiar to us; we don't have to consciously think, "First I open the door, then I sit down, then I close the door, then I put the key in the slot, then I turn the key, then the engine will make noise, then I put my foot on the brake, shift into reverse, and the car will start moving backward," and so on. We simply follow our script.

Although rational thinking is the antithesis of scripts, scripts do help us function efficiently in the world. If we were to "tell" someone who was not familiar with the restaurant script that John went to a restaurant for dinner, ordered lobster, paid the check, and left, he would not know what John ate for dinner. In this sort of situation, scripts are useful because no one wants to be neurotically analyzing every single event in life. We don't think much about restaurants, we know how they work, and we make assumptions about what happens in them. We allow scripts to substitute for thinking. This is appropriate because it makes living in the everyday world an easier task. What's bad is that scripts prevent us from asking questions and making educated guesses. When kids lock into their favorite scripts, they don't have to do the work analysis demands. When children watch lots of stupid, formulaic television shows, they don't analyze what they've watched. When kids go on the same vacation every year, they are following the vacation script and don't have to do much reasoning while they're sitting on the same beach building the same sandcastles. When an eighteen-year-old decides to major in biology and become a doctor because his father did the same thing, he's following a script and not analyzing his decision.

Scripts have tremendous power over all of us, but especially over children, including teenagers and young adults. A theater major in one of my classes one day announced that she had decided to become a lawyer. She was doing so because the career script she was operating under dictated that she do something sensible and choose a field that would allow her to capitalize on her dramatic skills. In her mind, being a lawyer was similar to being an actress; she would simply be performing in court rather than on a stage. This script prevented her from doing the necessary analysis. Influenced perhaps by television scripts (where lawyers are always involved in highly dramatic cases), she automatically assumed that there was a match between her talent and interests and the field of law. To challenge this assumption, I told everyone in the class of this student's new career choice and asked them if they thought this was a wise move. They unanimously agreed that it was a poor decision; they appreciated her dramatic flair but recognized that most lawyers spend most of their time enmeshed in boring detail work.

She had trouble seeing beyond her script. At Northwestern University, there are many theater majors like this student who are under the sway of another type of script. It prevents them from asking and analyzing the following question: Why are they majoring in theater? The script-based illogic is that you need a theater degree from a school like Northwestern to be a successful actor. The career script dictates that you need a degree in an area relevant to your chosen career. In fact, actors need nothing of the kind. They actually need experience in summer stock, in small theater groups, and in Hollywood, where they can master acting skills and develop the relationships that will lead to success. While some successful actors do indeed have theater degrees from prestigious schools, the majority do not. If you were to analyze how much a degree contributed to the success of a given actor, you would find that it contributed relatively little. We really learn from experience, not from class. Getting schools to provide experiences instead of lessons is not easy. Of course, some theater schools do exactly that, but the point is that the degree has no magic to it, and sound analysis would reveal this fact.

Scripts offer us the illusion of logic. When I was in school, I decided to become a chemical engineer because I liked chemistry and knew engineering involved math, at which I was proficient. I had not done the requisite analysis, and assumed that careers are exactly what they "sound" like. Finally I roused myself from this lazy thinking and actually got a book out of the library about chemical engineering. When I read it and learned that chemical engineering was about fluid flows in enormous vats, I decided to look for another major.

Four Ways to Stimulate Logical Thinking and Well-Reasoned Decisions

Raising an analytical kid may seem like more of a challenge than helping your child acquire qualities such as verbal facility or creativity. Many of you may decide that you're not particularly logical or that analysis is too complicated a skill for an ordinary parent to teach. In fact, just about anyone can help his children develop this skill as long as these guidelines are followed:

1. Put your children in complicated situations and ask them to reason their way out.

When I gave my son a map of the Paris Métro and said, "Figure out how to get around," I was doing just this. I'm not advocating throwing kids into situations that are so far beyond them that they'll just become frustrated and angry because they don't have a clue how to handle it. I knew my son was interested in subways and that he had the capability to determine how the Metro worked. If your child has an interest in a given area, she'll be motivated to figure out an answer to a problem. Don't underestimate your child's ability to deal with complexity. The challenge of an intricate situation starts the analytical wheels spinning. Place your child in a situation where she can't rely on a script. If she loves science, pose a scientific problem to her. It doesn't matter if you know the answer. Speculate together, then find out. Why is the sky blue? This actually is an interesting question.

Complicated situations can run the gamut. For a child interested in building things, get some Lego blocks and ask him to design the Frank Lloyd Wright building you saw the previous week. For a younger child fascinated by dinosaurs, you might ask her to draw pictures that show how and why dinosaurs became extinct. These situations will drive kids to ask questions, to make assumptions, and to test theories.

As you design these situations, however, here are two things to avoid:

1. *Anything boring.* Some of you will try so hard to challenge and confound your child that you'll forget to add the essential ingredient of fun. Just because it's an area of interest to your child doesn't automatically mean that it will be exciting or entertaining. You need to consider what turns your child on, what she finds fascinating. Then she'll be more than willing to do the hard work analysis requires.

2. *"Right answer" goals.* Schools are fixated on solving problems in order to get the right answers. In life, right answers don't always exist. For most problems, there are multiple solutions and a variety of ways to arrive at them. Analytical

thinking is developed from struggling with alternatives, not from choosing the right answer. In fact, as soon as you find the right answer, you stop thinking. Far better if children keep mulling over a situation and examining the alternatives. Therefore, don't design a situation where your child has to find the answer or where you terminate analysis by saying those devastating words, "That's the wrong answer." Who knows why the dinosaurs disappeared? There are all sorts of ways to interpret a Frank Lloyd Wright building in Lego blocks. Give your child a reasonable amount of thinking room in which to work.

2. Use the Socratic method to help them reason their way out of situations.

The Socratic method is derived from the story of Socrates' attempting to help a slave solve a mathematics problem. Socrates wanted to prove that all knowledge is innate, an absurd concept. What isn't absurd is the way Socrates asked questions of a slave, subtly helping him acquire the information he needed by asking questions in a certain way. To onlookers, it seemed as if this slave had actually found the answer to the math problem from within. In reality, Socrates had dropped just enough hints and compelled the slave to think through the problem so that he was able to reason out a solution.

Every parent can engage in Socratic dialogs with her child. The process is simply one of asking leading questions and breaking down a subject into more accessible parts. Go back to my story of when my son asked why Southeast Asian food was so hot. Rather than giving him the answer, I asked him what was the main trait of Southeast Asian countries. When he made a reasonable guess, I asked him what happened when it gets really hot. He figured out that these spices were useful as preservatives, but that wasn't the point. Even if he hadn't arrived at the right answer, he was learning to analyze rather than ignore or accept.

Phrase your questions as Socrates did, offering tidbits of information and directions to pursue that will help children investigate the matter at hand. Whatever you do, don't answer their questions directly. In fact, you don't have to know the answer. My daughter and I once went to Pompeii and stood at the remains of a wine stand, speculating together about where the wine may have come from, where it was stored, and so on. I had no more information about these issues than she did. In a sense, we had interchangeable roles—we each took turns playing Socrates and the slave.

You don't have to go to Pompeii to do this. Go in the backyard with your kid, find a gnarled old tree, and speculate on how it became so hunched and crooked.

3. Suggest complicated situations that kids can immediately relate to.

You may not be able to determine your child's area of interest, or your description of a given situation (too pedantic, too self-involved, too boring, etc.) may not spark his interest. If this happens, choose a situation that is obviously relevant, like dealing with a mean teacher or a dispute among friends. For instance: What would you do if Jerry told you he wanted to try out for the basketball team, and he plays the same position that you do; how might you handle this? Or: What happens if your best friend isn't invited to Jane's party and you are; what alternatives are available to you under these circumstances?

Social situations are just as useful as academic ones for enhancing analytical skills. Experience is experience is experience; you can reflect on and talk about one as well as another.

4. Start teaching them to analyze when they're one or two.

Analysis seems like such a grown-up concept that it's difficult to conceive of adolescents engaging in this process, let alone smaller children. Toddlers, however, are inveterate hypothesis-testers. There's a reason that kids stick their fingers in electric sockets and pull the dog's tail. They are always asking themselves: "What would happen if . . . ?" This is how analysis begins, and children at even very young ages do it reflexively.

You need to develop this reflex in more sophisticated ways. For instance, let's say you're playing catch with a small child. After throwing a ball back and forth a few times, use a bit of legerdemain and hide the ball in your pocket and ask, "What happened to the ball?" Most children will do things like asking you where the ball is or starting to search for it. When they find it, they'll ask you how you did what you did and then attempt to imitate your sleight of hand.

What you've done is violate the child's expectations, and expectation failure, as we know, is a learning catalyst. When the ball didn't return to the child as expected, he immediately began to investigate what had happened. Eventually, he reasoned that you hid the ball and fooled him. There should be a continuous verbal interchange between you and the child as he's trying to determine how you made the ball disappear. This demonstrates that dialog is the key to unraveling these mysteries.

The more complex the experiences you expose a small child to, the more she will become accustomed to analyzing. If you've always lived in the Midwest and gone to inland lakes, take a trip to the ocean and have your child dip a finger in the water and taste it. "How does it taste?" you might ask. "How is it different from the water back home?" "How would you get the salt out of the water, do you suppose?"

But What If I Don't Want to Raise a Coldly Analytical Kid?

I'm not suggesting that you attempt to create a little Mr. Spock; I wouldn't want to have an emotion-deficient child who makes every decision in his life without considering how he feels. Cool-headed reason, however, is a valuable component of practical intelligence, and it doesn't mean you can't also factor in how you feel about a decision. But we live in a society where feelings increasingly take precedence in decision-making. Listen to people talk and you'll be amazed at how many times they say things like "It just feels right." In a world that has become increasingly complex and confusing, people naturally rely on their scripts and don't do the sometimes daunting analytical work decision-making demands. As a parent, you need to arm your child with the analytical skills to deal with the complexity. At some point, your kid is going to be asked by a prospective employer why he wants to work for a given organization. What you don't want him to say is: "Oh, this company just feels right to me." Instead, you want him to share a cogent analysis of why there's a fit between who he is and what the organization stands for.

At the same time, children shouldn't discount that little voice inside their heads that seems to operate outside the realms of reason and logic. As a parent, you should raise your children to respect both their conscious and their unconscious knowledge. At times, this is a difficult distinction to make. It's sometimes tricky to distinguish between a child who is following a mindless script and one who is following an impulse that has a basis in fact. Religious zealots have no basis in fact for their beliefs. Neither do teenagers who refuse to take a job that interests them because "it seems dumb." But there are times when your decision-making is powerfully influenced by a feeling or instinct that seems to have "roots"; it's anchored in something solid, though you can't exactly pinpoint what it is.

Here's an example. I was traveling on a train in Holland, and as I was passing through Amersvoort I started thinking about a girl I knew in sixth grade with a Dutch last name, Naarden. I hadn't thought about her in years, but the name suddenly popped into my head. A few minutes later, the train passed through a town named Naarden. Now there are a variety of explanations for what happened. One explanation is that I'm psychic. Another is that this was pure coincidence, albeit a highly unlikely one. A third explanation is that I saw a sign saying the next town was Naarden or that in my travels I had somehow passed this way before. Since I couldn't recall having seen a sign, I tried to remember if I had taken this train before. Though I hadn't been on this specific train, I had been on another train in Holland, and it too had passed through Amersvoort. Suddenly, I realized that I had become aware of Naarden's location two years earlier and then had "forgotten" about it. That fact became part of my unconscious knowledge, summoned to consciousness when I passed through Amersvoort. On a conscious level, I wasn't aware that there was a town named Naarden or of its proximity to Amersvoort. Unconsciously, I did know these facts.

We don't know everything we know. For this reason, we need to heed strong impulses when we're pondering a decision. Though you can't teach your children how to make use of unconscious knowledge, you do want to encourage them to keep an open mind and not tune out that insistent little voice in their heads that seems to know more than they do.

Perhaps the best thing you can do is encourage them to analyze their impulses and feelings. If they say, "I want to be a psychologist because I'm good with people," challenge that vague assertion. Ask them questions that force them to define what they mean by "good with people." They may be right that psychology is a good profession for them, but they need to think through how their skills and interests dovetail with the requirements of a career in psychology.

Communicate to your kids that everything is open to analysis. You need to fight against the blind acceptance that is so prevalent in our society and that is inculcated by a school system that doesn't encourage kids to question and hypothesize. Children need to learn to ask why rather than just follow their scripts. Part of the reason they need to ask why is that these scripts are authored to some extent by parents. Kids unthinkingly copy the behaviors and attitudes of parents, and while this isn't always a bad thing, it's not conducive to analysis.

There is the story of the woman who always made a ham a certain way, slicing off one end of the ham before putting it in the oven to cook. Her daughter made ham exactly the same way. One day the daughter asked her mom why she cut off the end, and her mother said that was just the way you make ham. As her daughter continued to probe, the mom admitted that her own mother had taught her this technique. They decided to call the grandmother and ask her why ham was cooked this way, and the grandmother said her pan was always too small for the ham, so she had to cut part of it so it would fit.

Some imitated behaviors have more of a negative impact than a silly cooking technique, so encourage your children to ask why.

Of Course, Too Many Whys Will Drive You Crazy

"Because I told you so" is a common parental response to a child asking why. Sometimes you don't feel like making the effort to explain. Sometimes it's uncomfortable or difficult to answer a child's question. We don't always have the time to do so, but smart kids require smart answers in order to stay smart. If you don't think and respect their desire to think, then why should they bother? Thinking is hard work, and only stupid people believe otherwise.

This is one of the paradoxes of raising a smarter kid:

> *While everything is open to analysis, not everything will be analyzed.*

You need to achieve a balance. There are going to be times when every parent has to say, "I'll tell you when you're older" or "This isn't open for discussion." You need to recognize what you can tolerate, but you also need to tolerate a significant number of questions if you want your child to be adept at reasoning.

The analytical kid's favorite word is why (it's also an important word for inquisitive kids, as we'll see a bit later), and every time you hear it, you should be reassured that your child is practicing and perfecting her analytical skills. As vexing as it might be to have to constantly explain things, this stage will pass. As children become older, they internalize these analytical skills and begin asking questions of themselves. Over time, they'll develop the tools necessary for self-exploration and will no longer be as dependent on you for assistance in their efforts to analyze the world around them.

8

How to Raise a Kid with More Gumption

GUMPTION is a little trickier to define than our other five qualities. The dictionary definition of "initiative or resourcefulness, courage or spunk," suggests what I mean in a general sense but doesn't convey why it's such an important trait for a smarter kid.

To illustrate its importance, let's look at gumption from a real world perspective. I have worked with many graduate students over the years, and I've found that many of the brightest can't obtain their doctorates. They've been genetically endowed with brilliance, they have a love for their subject, and yet they come up short of a doctorate; they drop out to become cabdrivers, they are content with a master's degree, they do everything but their theses. The ones who do acquire doctorates and go on to successful academic careers are not any brighter than those who don't.

In many instances, the differentiating trait is gumption. Though a lack of ambition obviously also enters into the equation, many of these students are ambitious, at least in the sense that they *want* to do well in their careers. The problem is they can't act on that want. People who do act on it have the stick-to-itiveness to the point of obsession necessary to complete all the work necessary for this degree; they are willing to take a risk and try an innovative thesis topic that not only gains their professor's approval but becomes a solid job credential. Their gumption also entails a willingness to take criticism and persevere; they aren't deterred when a professor gives them a bad grade or when they hear about how tough it is for people in their field of study to find jobs.

My son demonstrated gumption in the fourth grade when he dressed in a coat and tie before the class election for president. I asked him why he was all dressed up, and he told me, "I'm looking for the girl vote." Certainly he knew that other kids would take shots at him for his appearance, but it didn't matter. Actually, it did matter, but he was willing to endure whatever sarcastic comments he received because he was driven to be class president and would do whatever it took to achieve that goal. What it took was gumption.

Gumption has many synonyms, including chutzpah, guts, and risk-taking. But what this trait really boils down to is a willingness to act on your beliefs and stick to your position, no matter what anyone else says or does. Gumption connotes action. It doesn't take place in someone's mind but requires expression in word or deed. Freud had lots of gumption. So did Che Guevera (gumption doesn't mean you're always right in your beliefs). The child who raises his hand and tells his teacher he disagrees with him has plenty of gumption because his teacher and the school system in general advocate conformity and quiescence above all else.

How Schools Beat the Gumption Out of Children

To be honest with you, I don't particularly like it when a student tells me that my ideas are wrong and that his are right. Ego alone causes a negative reaction, but beyond that is the larger issue of maintaining order and teaching the planned lesson. In the lower grades, this is the whole point. As we have seen, schools were founded to create docile factory workers. They evolved along the lines of a day care model and remain intent on producing upstanding citizens (who don't use drugs, have unprotected sex, commit crimes, or do any of the things health education is designed to prevent). If children were allowed to interrupt, say whatever was on their minds, and challenge authority, what kind of behavior would schools be endorsing? As teachers are fond of saying to unruly students, "If everyone talked out of turn as you do, how would we ever get anything done?"

If you don't conform in school, you're punished. I'm not simply talking about verbal reprimands and bad grades but humiliation. My gumption-minded son announced in seventh grade that he was in favor of the legalization of drugs. This position didn't sit well with his teacher or classmates—the school was caught up in just-say-no-to-drugs fever—and he was verbally attacked. Still, he refused to give an inch.

While there isn't a school policy prohibiting gumption, there are all sorts of unofficial policies that mitigate against it. Even in elementary school, children are talked out of their strongly held beliefs. Think about a child in third grade insisting that he believes in UFOs; the teacher certainly would try to convince him that this belief was wrongheaded, that most people don't subscribe to it, and that he may be watching too many movies about aliens. Kids know that they're going to get clobbered if they stand up for what they believe in when it goes against the grain; most of them know what teachers want them to say in class and in the papers they write, and they realize they'll be graded down if they take a contrary position. The reason given for their lower grade will be things like "You missed the point," "You're just being frivolous," or "There's no research to back up this conclusion." A very conservative mentality underlies what is taught in schools, not necessarily politically, but in terms of variation from the norm. What do you think would happen if a student argued that Shakespeare was an overrated writer? Or how would the administration react if someone insisted that he didn't have to take a foreign language because "I hate it, have no aptitude for it, and won't need it when I become a software developer after I drop out of school"? How would a teacher and a class respond if someone got up and announced that she found the politically correct curriculum limiting and wanted to read more books by dead white men?

I'm not arguing that any of these positions are right or wrong, just that it would require gumption to take them within the school environment. What's scary is that schools teach students the wrong lesson about gumption. They equate success with anticipating what the teacher wants and giving it to him; you receive good grades not for stubbornly articulating and sticking to your idiosyncratic position but for figuring out what the party line is and making it your own.

I've found that the best students often possess the least gumption. I have someone who works for me who went to the top schools and received the highest grades. You won't find many people with better academic records than she possesses, and she has been a terrific employee for many years. But she is someone who never would insist on pushing the company in a new direction or demand that she work on a particular project she believes in. She simply is highly effective in doing the tasks assigned to her. All this is fine, and I don't view her lack of gumption as a character flaw. It does, however, limit her achievement in the world, and I blame the schools for this. Though she may simply not have had the type of personality gumption requires (an issue we'll address a bit later), she was the classic high achiever in school and moderate achiever in the professional world; her school experiences conditioned her to keep her gumption at bay.

Three Traits of Highly Gumptious People

Gumption is a many-faceted concept, but for our purposes here, let's talk about three qualities that are essential for gumption:

1. A willingness to break the rules.
2. Single-mindedness.
3. Self-confidence.

Successful entrepreneurs, pioneering scientists, and other high-achieving professionals break the rules not because they're anarchists but because they feel the old rules don't work as well as the new ones they've created. They first evaluate the rules, decide which ones are viable and which ones are not, and invent new ones to replace the latter. This is the process you need to teach your children. In a sense, you want them to learn how to break rules intelligently. You want them to understand that if they break certain rules, they will cause harm to themselves or others. If they become tremendously drunk and drive a car, they will be breaking rules in a stupid manner. Having a drink with dinner and then driving home, however, is breaking a rule intelligently. As long as they've learned that their driving ability isn't diminished by one drink, then there's no harm in breaking this rule.

You want your kids to get in the habit of breaking rules. Rules represent limits, and progress is made when limits are removed or pushed outward. Be forewarned, however, that this isn't an easy concept to implement. In high school, my daughter once told me that she was sleeping over at a friend's house and her friend told her parents that she was sleeping over at our house. What they and other kids were actually doing was renting a hotel room and drinking. Naturally, I was upset with my daughter when I discovered this ruse and let her know it. I told her I was disappointed that she had lied to me, and I admitted that if she had told me the truth about what she and her friends intended to do, I wouldn't have allowed it. If I recall correctly, I believe I gave her a mild punishment for breaking the rule about lying. What I did not do was make her feel that she was a jerk for lying or that she had done something that had diminished her forever in my eyes. Kids expect to be punished when they break rules (just as entrepreneurs expect to be punished financially when their precedent-setting ventures fail). But when the punishment becomes personal—when you make your child feel as if breaking a rule was akin to committing a capital crime—then you make them reluctant to break any rules.

Single-mindedness is also sometimes difficult for parents to countenance. When your child becomes obsessed with one thing and ignores other subjects or even other people to pursue it, your inclination is to say, "You need to diversify your interests." In fact, becoming deeply and single-mindedly involved in an interest is crucial to gumption. My son was obsessively interested in subways for years, and it led him to his career. Such obsessive behavior may not make sense to parents or may seem a big investment in a trivial subject, but it's how kids develop expertise. The well-diversified child simply knows a little bit about a lot of things; the single-minded child becomes an expert.

This leads us to our third aspect of gumption: self-confidence.

Expertise bequeaths self-confidence to kids. When they know a subject intimately, they're much more willing to take risks within that subject area, to speak their minds and stand up for themselves. It's much easier to withstand the criticism that comes to those with gumption because you know you're right. Or at the very least, you know you know more than everyone else about a given topic. And even if you're ultimately wrong, your self-confidence allows you to take action. In every class, there are a number of very bright kids who know the answers but never say anything. As certain as they are of the answers, they're not certain of themselves. They're often generalists rather than single-subject experts, and that's why they lack the gumption to risk raising their hands and making a mistake.

Gumption-Building Tactics

Here are three things every parent can do to increase the odds of bringing out the gumption in their children.

First, encourage your child to run for class office. Most kids don't want to do this; the prospect of having to brag about themselves, to make a speech, to expose themselves to losing, and to be elected to a position of responsibility is not particularly enticing. But taking the risk and trying to obtain a leadership position is a great way to develop gumption. It doesn't matter if your child wins or loses. When my son got dressed up and ran for class president in fourth grade, he lost the election. Years later, he was elected president of his fraternity. I'm convinced that he would never have won that office if he hadn't demonstrated some gumption early on.

Give your kids a push in this direction (after all, Joe Kennedy certainly pushed his sons toward elective office). Speak enthusiastically about the possibility; ask them what they would do if they were class president and how they might change things to make the class more fun or a better place to learn. Make it a fun activity to create campaign posters and slogans, and make sure they understand that you don't particularly care if they win or lose the election, as long as they experience the process.

Second, send your child to summer camp. Let me be more specific. Certain types of camps—computer camps, science camps, and so on—are often nothing more than classrooms transferred to prettier environments. They consist largely of one lecture or seminar after another. While they may help build expertise in a subject, they don't provide kids with the freedom necessary for gumption to flower. Summer camp takes place outside, and we're much less restrictive with children when it comes to outdoor activities. Camps gives kids a chance to get into trouble, to have adventures, to be on their own. It is a risky environment, not physically as much as emotionally. Though there are counselors, they often know enough to stay out of their campers' hair. As a result, kids have the opportunity to be leaders, to invent games, and to pull all sorts of original stunts.

Camp is the last bastion of the unprogrammed child. So many children rocket from one planned activity to the next and are never allowed to act autonomously—or to show much initiative outside of very narrow boundaries. Years ago, kids got together on their own and invented secret societies and went roaming around the neighborhood investigating and speculating. If you live in a suburb, the odds are that on a nice weekend morning you won't find a kid in sight; they're confined to a variety of programmed activities.

Third, sign up both your boys and your girls for sports. As much as kids' soccer is a planned activity, there's plenty of room within the game for children to be leaders and heroes. Watch any game and you'll see children take a chance, miss a kick, save a goal, sacrifice their scoring to play defense, try a fancy, completely original move to get past a defender, and so on.

As I've emphasized earlier, sports are the perfect place for children to experience failure, and gumption flows from failure. Striking out in a big game is tremendously disappointing, but there are very few children who strike out and refuse to play baseball again. Most are eager and willing to keep playing because they've discovered that they're strong enough to survive their failures. They're also curious about why they failed when they expected to get a hit; they're motivated to practice harder in order to do better next time. All this makes it easier for them to exhibit gumption and get up and risk striking out again, not only in baseball but in other areas of life. As you probably noticed, failure is a likely outcome of running for office or going to camp. Kids frequently don't win elections and boys get lost in the woods when they attempt to find the girls' camp a few miles down the road.

Does Your Child Have It or Does He Need to Develop It?

To a certain extent, gumption is innate. Some babies are born squirming about, and soon they're itching to escape their cribs. When they're toddlers, they seem willing to take any risk in their exploration. Many times, these kids exhibit gumption at an early age; they're the ones who are often obsessively focused on a particular idea or interest throughout their lives. Given that Bill Clinton wanted to be president since he was a teenager, it's not too much of a stretch to conclude that he was probably born with gumption.

If you have a child like this, you don't need to do much except leave him alone. Unfortunately, schools and parents conspire to diminish or eliminate the gumption in these types of kids. They tell them not to be so obsessive and come down hard on them for being so obstinate and narrow in their interests. Ritalin and verbal and physical abuse are all methods that can take gumption out of a child. If you're the parent of a gumptious child, all you really need to do is teach her to pick her spots. If she's single-minded about everything and breaks every rule she can find, that's a problem, especially during adolescence. The trick here is to help her to know when gumption is called for and when it's not worth the hassle that will ensue. Essentially, what she needs to learn is judgment, and you can help her learn it by letting her talk to you and reflect on the unpleasant consequences of breaking certain types of rules or being bullheaded about certain types of things. Remember, learning happens when you have a lot of experiences you can reflect on and talk about—experiences where expectation failure takes place. When she tells you she didn't realize that refusing to do a homework assignment she found demeaning would result in her suspension from school, she's unconsciously indexing this experience and will be able to recall it the next time she's in a similar situation.

If, on the other hand, you have a shy, unassertive child who rarely if ever exhibits gumption, then you need to encourage him to break a rule, be single-minded, and develop an area of expertise that will produce self-confidence. My son, despite his eagerness to run for fourth-grade class president and his single-minded interest in subways, sometimes didn't show gumption in school situations. I used to ask him why he followed every rule in school but was perfectly willing to break the few rules I had. "I'm not afraid of you," he told me. When I asked him why he was afraid of the teacher, my son explained that the teacher might not like him or might give him a bad grade if he were to do something wrong. I told him that at one point or another, he was going to have to stand up to the teacher when his view ran counter to the teacher's rules (which he did when he took his legalization-of-drugs stance in seventh grade).

Standing up to authority figures (besides parents) is something that you can urge your kid to do. Let him know that you'll support him if he does so; talk to him about what rule he feels is unfair or what he wants to spend more time on (and a teacher won't let him). I don't want to make it sound like exhibiting gumption in these situations is easy for shy, unassertive kids. Their personalities combined with their fear of teachers and peer pressure to conform are formidable obstacles. But if the motivation is strong enough, children will be able to overcome these obstacles. You need to help them locate the particular interest or topic that consumes them, that really gets them wound up and excited. Even the quietest, most unassuming children can be motivated to defy authority in defense of this interest. When boys and girls develop a strong point of view—when they are emotionally and intellectually invested in a given subject—they naturally want to fight for their belief. Rather than defy authority out of mindless rebellion, these kids are defying it based on knowledge, interest, and personal perspective. When kids discover what's worth showing gumption about, they're often willing to endure reprimands by teachers and mockery from classmates. A child with gumption possesses the resilience necessary to endure everything from taunts to threats in order to achieve his goal.

Let Your Child See Your Gumption

Parents with gumption often raise children who possess this quality. This is partly because of the genetic predisposition I noted earlier but also because of observed behavior. Gumption in action is usually memorable. When a child observes a parent standing up to a police officer and steadfastly denying he was speeding, it is an impactful moment. When a kid sees his mom working the phones, knocking on doors, and making speeches in order to be elected to the school board, he witnesses a display of gumption.

Some parents are reluctant to let their children see them acting in gumptious ways. They harbor the mistaken notion that it's not good for kids to see them breaking the rules or that there's something unattractive about a single-minded devotion to a cause or goal. "I don't want my kid to be as neurotically obsessed as I am," more than one highly successful parent has said. Many times, however, "neurotic obsession" is merely hyperbole, and the behavior being described is stick-to-itiveness.

Gumption isn't always pretty. When you take risks and fail, your words and actions may not always be attractive; you may curse, rail against your enemies, and do or say things that Ozzie and Harriet would never do or say. But as long as your child also sees you move past your anger, rebound from your failure, and focus on the task at hand, then you'll impart an important lesson about gumption. I exposed my children to my single-minded, rule-breaking, self-confident behaviors both at home and at work. They were aware of my willingness to test "odd" ideas like trying to get computers to understand English, my persistence in doing so, my failures when experiments didn't turn out well, and the criticism I received for spending all this time on what others in the field viewed as heresy. They were able to observe that my gumption didn't result in any serious damage and that it sometimes produced a variety of rewards.

If a child is the first one in his family to exhibit gumption, that's difficult. If a parent sets the precedent, it's infinitely easier.

Gumption Is Nothing More Than a Dream Pursued

Gumption is fueled by a dream. You need a powerful reason to exhibit pigheadedness, to take risks, and to rebound from failures. "Goal" is too mild a word to describe this fuel; it suggests a desirable outcome rather than one that is the culmination of a vision. One of my dreams, for instance, is to fix the schools. I am driven by a vision of schools as a place where real learning takes place. As a result, I am willing to spend a great deal of time working on visionary educational software that no one may ever use; I am willing to engage in debates with traditional educators who criticize my ideas; and I am willing to give talks and write articles and books on the subject. I may not be able to fix the schools, but I will have many valuable experiences along the way. When you're single-minded in your pursuit of a dream, you usually make a number of productive discoveries. When I was attempting to teach computers to understand English, some of the knowledge gained from these experiments ultimately made its way into the design of Internet search engines. There are many stories of scientists diligently looking for one thing, only to discover something else.

Foster your child's interesting dreams. Interesting dreams are often outsized and idiosyncratic, reflecting the uniqueness of your child. They can range from wanting to be a synchronized swimmer in the Olympics to wishing to sing *La Traviata* at the Met to aspiring to be a world-famous clothing designer. Uninteresting dreams, on the other hand, are mundane and small. If your child dreams of dropping out of school and watching television all day or says he wants to become a corporate lawyer, I would question whether these dreams are worth pursuing. Interesting dreams sometimes are impossible dreams. Even if this is the case, don't discourage your child. Help her understand what she has to do if she wants to fulfill this dream, ask her questions about it, and let her experiment. On the path to the dream, she'll end up in all sorts of unfamiliar situations that will result in learning. The original dream will probably sidetrack into a variety of other dreams before she finds one that is more readily achievable.

Dreams are powerful stuff, the magic ingredient in gumption. If your child has a dream, he will go after it with great tenacity. He may not achieve the dream, but he will achieve many other things along the way.

9

How to Raise a More Ambitious Kid

AMBITION may seem like a strange trait to include in a book about raising smarter children, but it makes sense when you remember that we're talking about practical intelligence. Like the stick-to-itiveness gumption provides, ambition is crucial if you want your child to be a successful adult.

What does your child want to be? Even if your child is only three or four years old, she's quite capable of ambition. I've talked to children this age who have told me they wanted to be firemen, astronauts, doctors, lawyers, and a variety of silly things (my son at two wanted to be "a mother"; I quickly disabused him of this notion, so he settled on football player). Kids may not grow up to be what they say they want to be, but the impulse is there to be something. What you don't want is to ask a kid what he hopes to be when he grows up and receive a blank look or a shrug. I was very happy that my daughter wanted to be president of the United States when she was little, even though the odds may have been against her. I nurtured this idea, encouraging her to think and talk about it. In a sense, she was practicing being ambitious, and practice is integral to any learning experience.

Perhaps more so than any of the other traits we've discussed, ambition is one that parents can bestow on their children through modeling the right attitudes and behaviors. Before discussing how this modeling works, let's define ambition.

Ambition Is Neither Blind Nor Ruthless

Ambition involves setting goals and working hard to achieve them. It is about wanting to be successful at something. You can be ambitious about anything, from making money to becoming an expert in an area of interest to being a great parent. Subjectively, we all value certain goals above others. I've never been particularly interested in materialistic goals; someone else may not be concerned with career goals.

To a certain extent, you need to be open-minded about the goals your child chooses. Certainly you want to discourage him from choosing a goal that violates your values or beliefs; you don't want your kid to be a drug dealer or a thief. But it's important to recognize that your child's ambition should flow from his natural areas of interest. If he loves playing with blocks and building elaborate structures, he may express a desire to be an architect. When you see a goal emerge from an interest, treasure it, nurture it, support it in every way possible.

Ambition has received a bad rap in our society. In some people's minds, it connotes greed, ruthlessness, and out-of-control egotism. This definition, however, is about ambition taken to an extreme. Extremely ambitious people may not care about whom they hurt and will gladly sacrifice friends and family to make a certain amount of money or achieve a powerful position.

While ambition does require tradeoffs, it does not require selling your soul to the devil. When you think about ambition, consider it in less extreme terms. If you view it as a Faustian pact, you'll become alarmed when your child begins working with great zeal to achieve a goal. With this alarm in your voice, you'll tell her she needs to develop other interests and shouldn't spend all her time and energy on this one pursuit; you'll suggest that she "let other kids have a chance" or that she's being "self-centered." In short, you'll overreact to what is really healthy ambition that requires great focus and hard work.

Ambition is concerned with setting standards for excellence, the achievement of which demands significant time and effort. It's also about getting what you want out of life and doing so in a self-chosen field and on your own terms. As a parent, you can help turn this definition of ambition into a reality for your child by modeling this behavior in your own life.

The Power Parents Possess

In the deepest sense of the term, ambition is an attempt to please one's parents. Consciously or not, we seek our parents' approval. One of the saddest things about the death of parents is that we no longer have anyone to cheer us on, to compliment us on our triumphs and encourage us to do more. One of the payoffs of working round the clock to become a doctor, lawyer, or other type of professional is hearing your parents tell you how proud they are of your accomplishment.

Because of this, parents can say and do things that influence both a child's level of ambition and what he's ambitious about. I remember being with my cousin when we were around eleven or twelve, and some family member asked him what he wanted to be. He said he didn't want to be much of anything because he knew I was the smart one in our family and that he assumed I'd be rich and he would live off me. My cousin chose to be a dentist like his father and opened a practice in the same town in which his father practiced. There is nothing wrong with this choice; it's just not an overly ambitious one. Without clear goals, children often end up copying parents' career choices, assuming this will meet with their approval. While this can lead to satisfying lives and careers, many times people find themselves in jobs they don't particularly like or find meaningful and can't quite figure out what's wrong. What's wrong is when children live out their parents' aspirations.

This isn't to say that my parents encouraged me from a very young age to be an ambitious academic. My father, however, clearly and frequently communicated that he wanted me to do better than he had. He didn't feel he had been very successful and wanted more for his son. Whenever things weren't going well for me and he knew about it, he'd accuse me of turning out like him. My mother's insistent message was that ambition equaled money; she was concerned that I find a job and a career where I could make a decent income. Somehow, these complex, mixed messages led me to a career that helped me gain the approval of both my mom and my dad.

While they didn't use the power they had to make me an ambitious kid on a conscious level, that was the net result. I'm suggesting here that you go about this business in a more purposeful manner. Specifically, send the following message to your child:

I'm equalable and beatable.

When you do activities with your children—playing games, sports, music, or whatever it happens to be—make sure they understand that they can be as good as and probably better than you. When you play one-on-one basketball with your son, let him know that if he keeps practicing, he'll probably be able to beat you. If your daughter is impressed by your dexterity as you work together on a model airplane, make it clear to her that someday she'll be able to do the same thing.

You plant the seed of ambition when children believe that if they work a little harder and do a bit more, they can achieve most any goal. This motivational magic turns a child into "the little engine that could," able to make it to the top of whatever hill he chooses to climb. I was very clear with my son about the sports I thought he could be better at than I. I identified the areas (like music) where I was bereft of talent and where he could certainly be more proficient than I. By doing so, you're giving your child a formula for success. In the Jewish tradition, it is believed that the next generation should be more successful than the previous one, and this belief is communicated in many different ways. This legacy compels Jewish children to use their skills to achieve ambitious objectives.

The opposite of this approach is to convince a child that he's never going to equal your success and talents. When you play a game, crush him. When you talk about an issue, belittle his intelligence. Tell him he's just a kid and too young to grasp the significance of an article you wrote or a speech you gave. Such messages nip ambition in the bud.

Realistic Goals

Most of you probably innately understand that it's foolish to tell your child what to be ambitious about. Nonetheless, some parents try to dictate careers to their child. While they may stop short of telling him outright that he should be a doctor, they may communicate that being a doctor is what's expected of him and anything less will meet with their disapproval. There are many young people in this world laboring at jobs that are prestigious and high-paying but that make them miserable. In many cases, the problem can be traced back to pleasing their parents.

At the same time, you can have a leveling influence on what they're ambitious about. Children are notoriously unrealistic about their career goals. When they're little, that's fine. But when they're a bit older, you may want to step in if your child is ambitious in one or both of the following ways:

1. Expresses a need to be the absolute best in a given area and is terribly dissatisfied and unhappy when he's not.
2. Aspires to a career or job where the odds of success are poor—rock star, politician, actor, astronaut, and so on.

In terms of the former, it's important to teach a child to aim high but not too high. A perfectionist mentality doesn't allow for failure, and failure, as we know, is a key component of learning. Kids who are ambitious to the nth degree will become frustrated when their expectations fail. Instead of rebounding from that failure with questions and a desire to try again, they'll become dispirited. Even if they achieve their ambitions in one sense, they'll never achieve them in another. Your child may become a heart surgeon, but she won't be the best heart surgeon in the world. If you'll recall, one part of our definition of ambition is "getting what you want out of life." These kids grow up never getting what they want.

Similarly, some children set their sights on glamorous jobs that are very difficult to secure. The classic case is a child who dreams of being a professional basketball player. I'm not saying that you should discourage your child from this goal, only that you give him a realistic sense of what attaining this type of goal involves.

You can help him develop this sense by creating what I have dubbed "goal-based scenarios." I've employed these scenarios for both adults and children in computer simulations designed to help them acquire specific knowledge and skills. The simulations place them in realistic situations in which they're motivated to solve a problem; the process of solving the problem gives them the experience and expectation failure necessary for learning.

You can do the same thing with your child. If your child wants to be a rock star, buy him a book about the lives of rock musicians and what they went through to succeed. Encourage him to form his own rock band with friends and try out for school and other music competitions. When he's older, encourage him to apply for a job at a local music store that sells guitars and drums to local musicians; he'll meet people trying to be rock stars and they can share their experiences with him. All this will give him a strong dose of reality and may cause him to modify his ambition so it's more achievable (or it may cause him to become ambitious about something else).

The other thing you can do—especially if your kid wants to be the absolute best—is model nonperfectionist behavior. How do you respond if you don't get that promotion you'd been hoping for? What do you say at the dinner table about criticism you received at the office earlier in the day? How do you act when you don't win your weekly tennis match? If you throw tantrums when you don't come in first or when everything doesn't go perfectly at work, your child will pick up on this cue. What you really want to teach him is that it's fine to express disappointment when things don't work out as you expected, but expressing constant fury and bitterness is counterproductive.

Take Advantage of Natural Ambition

Children are born with different temperaments, but all kids will be ambitious if given half a chance. You can do many things to bring out—or stifle—this ambition from childhood to young adulthood. Here are some do's and don'ts:

1. Do teach your child to read as early as possible. As I've emphasized earlier, you shouldn't feel constrained by the notion that you're being "pushy" by teaching your child reading before she enters school. This is one of a child's first significant accomplishments. She learns that if she works hard, fails frequently, and keeps practicing, she can achieve this goal. Not only that, but she's achieving it on her own rather than as part of a large classroom group, demonstrating the viability of self-learning and one-on-one learning. Without exception, every child I've observed who has mastered reading on her own has gained a tremendous sense of power, tangibly grasping the rewards that come with achieving an ambition.

2. Do push your child to do sports as early as possible. Unless your kid is completely uncoordinated or has no interest in sports, make an effort to play catch, shoot baskets, go to the ice rink, ski, and kick around a soccer ball with your child. Something is bound to capture his interest and give him a goal to shoot for. Again, this gives kids a chance to achieve a significant ambition. My daughter has never forgotten when she hit a home run with the bases loaded in the bottom of the ninth. Sports provides countless opportunities for practice, failure, and a wide range of goals—from mastering a skill to becoming an all-state player.

3. Don't be negative or defeatist in front of your children. Try to maintain an optimistic, can-do attitude. Children need to feel there's a point to their ambitious feelings, that the practice and hard work necessary to achieve a goal are worth it. If you're constantly telling them what a tough world it is out there and complaining that some people get all the breaks, you will dull their ambitious edge.

4. Do give your children something to be ambitious about. When you recognize that your son or daughter demonstrates interest in and aptitude for something, capitalize on it. I've seen parents who, upon recognizing that their child has developed an interest in a subject, expect this interest to blossom on its own. While this can happen, you can accelerate the process by directing the interest. If your child likes fiddling around on the computer, research and purchase new programs that will challenge him. If your child enjoys drawing, sign her up for lessons (one-on-one lessons rather than group lessons that end up replicating a classroom environment). Investing time and money in an interest will pay off down the road.

5. Don't make ambition into an oppressive exercise. Let's say your kid loves reading. Don't quiz him on what he's read; don't berate him for missing the main point of a story; don't insult him by telling him he's reading the wrong types of books; don't make a checklist of books he has to read. You may sincerely believe that your checklists and criticisms will help him improve his reading. In fact, you're making the process tedious and boring, while learning should be fun. While ambition translates into hard work, it should be enjoyable hard work.

6. Do take your children to work (but don't do it unless you let them see you in action). Most people respond to "take your daughter/son to work" day by giving their kids a highly filtered view of themselves in work situations. My father once took me to work with him, and I never saw what he actually did for a living; most of the time was spent using chairs with rollers as a form of locomotion. Your kids need to see you interacting with other people: asking and answering questions, making decisions, debating points. I've taken my children to see me lecture as well as to the office, where they've seen me coming up with ideas. You need to model in a very tangible way what success looks like.

7. Don't panic when your child becomes an unambitious adolescent. Although adolescence is only a phase, it will come as a bit of a shock when your teenager suddenly loses interest in the goals you've encouraged for years. Teenagers, who naturally rebel against everyone, focus on ambition as a convenient target for their rebellion, especially if their parents think it is a worthy attribute. Teenagers may hold on to other, smarter kid traits such as being more verbal or creative, but ambition is one that they may forsake temporarily. There's not much you can do except wait this one out.

8. Don't make them afraid to try new things. When my children were little, my wife and I took them sledding. As we were going down the hill for the first time, my wife fell off the sled, hurt her leg, and began to complain about the pain. Her complaints were understandable but unfortunately timed since they came during a new experience for our children. The inadvertent message her complaints sent them was that (1) sledding is dangerous and therefore should be avoided; (2) any new experience should be feared. (As it turned out, my wife had a good reason to complain, since she had broken her leg.) While it's not always possible to hide your negative reaction to a new experience, you should try whenever possible to communicate that such an experience should be embraced. Fear is an obstacle to ambition. When parents communicate this fear—when they tell kids that it's dangerous to play a sport or that they can't read a book because it's too difficult—they're encouraging them to play it safe and not try anything new or different. Ambitious kids work hard at what interests them, and they work at it in different ways. They keep trying new and increasingly difficult projects related to their interest, and they're not afraid to fail.

9. Do be there and be fair. Absentee parents and aggressively critical parents tend to produce unambitious children. When parents aren't there, kids don't receive clear messages about what will please Mom and Dad. When parents are jerks, children lack the supportive environment they need to risk failure. Spending time with your kids and being civil and reasonable are simple measures that foster ambition.

Natural Versus Artificial Goals

School warps a child's sense of ambition. Perfect attendance, receiving top grades, scoring well on standardized tests, and getting into Harvard are artificial goals. They make sense to schools because they help keep order and make things manageable. There's a logic (albeit an artificial logic) to how schools are run, and there are clear standards and measures, facilitating assessment of both students and teachers.

All this results in a definition of ambition that doesn't jibe with the real world. You need to be ambitious about something you care about and that has meaning in your life. Achieving a meaningful goal provides a deep sense of fulfillment. Receiving an A in a biology class you care nothing about provides the most shallow form of fulfillment. The danger is that students confuse real and false ambition; they believe they've achieved something meaningful when they get that acceptance notice from a top school in the mail, when all they've really done is played the game according to the rules.

If schools wanted to encourage natural ambition, they would allow children to set goals they really cared about. One student would spend the semester reading every James Bond book. Another would work at mastering a difficult Mozart piece on the violin. A third would spend months in the science lab attempting to produce a complex chemical reaction. A fourth would listen to every Beastie Boys CD and memorize all the lyrics. These goals all flow from a child's interest, and they would be self-determined and largely self-achieved (with a teacher acting as guide and mentor). Of course, allowing children to follow their natural ambitions would create considerable chaos in the school system, and it would be difficult if not impossible to grade students on the same scale.

I don't want to overstate my case and claim that all schools prevent all students from following their natural ambitions. In the areas of music, art, and sports, some students are allowed to set goals that relate to their real areas of interest. Some progressive schools also allow students to set their own goals (though my experience is that many of these schools clearly communicate to students what goals are worth achieving and thereby taint the process).

Most children, however, are denied the opportunity to pursue their true goals and develop the type of ambition that I'm advocating. This problem isn't completely the fault of the schools. Our culture reinforces the notion that grades, degrees, and prestigious schools are the only indices of success. There is a television commercial in which a man who cleans pools for a living receives a twenty-year-old telegram indicating that he was accepted at Harvard. The implication is that if he had received the telegram on time, he would be successful and not relegated to the lowly task of cleaning pools. Still, the message is clear: Schools are the gateway to goal achievement.

They're not, and ambitious kids interested in computers are demonstrating that fact. Not only are admissions to computer science graduate schools down, but many of the best and brightest students are dropping out before receiving their undergraduate degrees. They're highly ambitious people driven by their own creative ideas, and they've formed innovative companies that are doing very well. They're proving that degrees often don't matter, and it seems likely that other students in other disciplines will follow their lead.

I'm not suggesting that you tell your kids to drop out of school. What I am proposing is that you nurture your child's goal-setting ability outside of school so that he can be ambitious about something he truly cares about.

Pipe Dreams and Paranoia

Adults who aren't satisfied with their work or feel they haven't achieved much complain constantly about unfair systems, the connections they lack, and how bosses play favorites. Others sit around and dream about what might be or what might have been. Go to any party and you'll find someone whining about his job or his career. Many of these people grew up not knowing what they wanted to do as adults. Or they were raised wanting what their parents wanted for them. Or they thought success would come easily—they received great grades and constant praise from parents no matter what they did.

You need to put your child in situations that teach him that success requires a lot of hard work and that he needs to be resilient when he fails. If you don't encourage goal-setting related to his interests—or if you provide empathy rather than a forward push when he fails—he will probably lack meaningful ambitions. As early as possible, you want to show him that significant accomplishments do not proceed in a straight line from wish to achievement. Along the way are a lot of unforeseen experiences, disappointing failures, opportunities for self-reflection, and time-consuming practice.

You can do this quite simply: Model the process of being ambitious. Don't hide your success from your kids, and don't make it seem easier than it was. Let them see you struggle with a work problem, express disappointment when things don't work out and happiness when you achieve what you wanted. There are parents whose children have absolutely no idea what they do and how they do it. Be a parent whose child is acutely aware of your goals and your struggles to achieve them.

10

How to Raise a More Inquisitive Kid

INQUISITIVENESS is the natural state of being alive. Human beings and animals are innately curious. The same impulse that causes babies to examine every inch of their cribs prompts puppies to sniff every new object they encounter. While this inquisitiveness can be annoying and even dangerous, it's also a building block of intelligence. The desire to explore and understand is what drives people to test theories, investigate alternatives, and come up with new ideas. Your child will have difficulty mastering a given subject or field without curiosity. It entices him to know more and thus be able to do more. Most experts are intensely and relentlessly curious.

If inquisitiveness is innate, why bother worrying about it? Won't inquisitiveness blossom in all children as they find their areas of interest? Not necessarily. School, parents, television, and other factors can conspire to create startlingly incurious children.

Before they even get out of grammar school, their inherent curiosity is stifled. Rather than asking questions about subjects that formerly interested them, they exhibit the same dull-witted passivity as when they're watching television.

The good news is that not only can parents prevent this from happening but they can provide children with many opportunities to exercise and develop their inquisitiveness.

Forms of Curiosity

Children are tremendously curious about a wide variety of subjects. If you took a class of twenty-five first-graders and researched what really turned them on, you'd find that each boy and girl has a burning desire to know more about something. One child may be curious about birds, another might have all sorts of questions about the planets, and a third might be fascinated by cars. On a more general level, we know the areas that children are eager to explore and learn about: why people treat them the way they do, their own bodies, sports, how to make things, drawing, music, and so on. Very few children, however, are naturally curious about the subjects school forces them to learn. Most kids don't have an intense curiosity about Dickens, state capitals, or algorithms.

When I was fourteen years old, my mother went to a school open house where my biology teacher told her that I was a very smart student but never asked any questions, implying that there must be something wrong with me. In fact, biology bored me and I had no desire to learn anything about unicelled animals. Why should I have had questions about something that didn't remotely interest me at the time?

This is the problem with school and curiosity. Most kids only ask questions about the subjects they're being taught out of a sense of "duty" or because they're worried they'll be criticized or down-graded, not because they're really curious about the answers. In fact, school tends to answer questions kids don't have rather than the ones they really want answered. When you don't have questions about a subject, you don't learn. You simply memorize, take the test, and forget.

Heartfelt questions, then, are a manifestation of inquisitiveness. When your child starts asking you a million questions about a specific topic, this identifies a real area of interest. The fact that he's curious about something weird or trivial—why cats land on their feet when dropped off the balcony, or the smell, texture, and taste of coffee beans—is neither here nor there. No matter where curiosity originates, it's a valid starting point, which as we'll see can lead to other, more "useful" areas of inquiry.

Questions, however, aren't the only form curiosity takes. People express their curiosity through different behaviors. A teenager, for instance, might drive fast because he's curious about how fast his car can go. A younger kid is curious about what will happen if he invites the new student to his house for lunch. A chemist is curious about what might happen if he mixes the liquids in test tubes X and Y. A kid is curious about what might happen if he fixes his best friend up with the girl who sits next to him in math class. Picasso was one of the most curious of modern artists, constantly experimenting with his painting techniques. In a very real sense, inquisitiveness involves experimentation. Like scientists, curious people are fascinated to see "what would happen if . . ." An avant-garde musician experiments with different tonalities and instruments in the same way a small child experiments with different types of balls to see how they bounce.

Curiosity is a curious thing, especially when we probe beneath the surface of our questions and behaviors and see how it helps us learn.

How the Curious Mind Works

When do children ask questions about things they're really interested in? When does their inquisitiveness reach such a fever pitch that they just have to find out the answer?

When their expectations fail.

Show me a child who never takes risks and does only what he can succeed at and I'll show you an incurious kid. When things go wrong—when you expect A and get B—you naturally seek an explanation, usually by asking a question. When you receive your explanation, you immediately ask another question: *If the explanation works in this situation, will it work in another situation?* As you're investigating this question, you're reminded of a related experience from the past and wonder if the explanation was valid in that case. From all this, you draw a conclusion that is essentially a new expectation of how the world works. And of course, your expectation soon fails, starting this "understanding" cycle all over again.

Let's look at this process within the context of memory. Curious people are able to store and retrieve their experiences from memory more easily than others. Here's why. We all have gigantic memories filled with facts, ideas, things we experienced, and stories we've heard. Memories, however, aren't static; they aren't infinite filing cabinets where our experiences are housed whole and unchanging. In fact, they change all the time. We need to adapt our memories because a startling new fact contradicts an old assumption or because an interesting new experience catalyzes a fresh generalization. This is how we learn and grow.

Let's say a child is sitting in a room and someone who is eight feet tall walks in. This is a startling new fact, an interesting experience, a clear expectation failure. The child may have been cognitively aware that there were people in the world who were eight feet tall, but it's the experience of actually seeing such a person that kick-starts his curiosity. He never expected to see such extreme height with his own eyes; he didn't anticipate how gigantic the person would be, especially compared to him; he didn't expect that it would be so difficult for this person to fit through the doorway or find a comfortable place to sit. This boy's curiosity causes him to ask questions about how things are built for people of different heights and weights; he starts wondering how people design airplanes, houses, and cars given the wide disparity in heights and weights; his memory is in a frenzied state of storing, retrieving, and adapting all the explanations he finds and subsequently has to reshape when they fail to meet certain expectations. Look at all the issues a curious kid can find to think about when stimulated to do so.

Sometimes, such curiosity continues for a long time indeed. A child starts with such an experience and decides to major in design and engineering in college, becoming highly proficient because of all that his intense curiosity has helped him learn (and store retrievably in his memory). This is how engineers are made. With curiosity, one thing leads to another and what might start out as a simple question ends up as a meaningful career.

But curiosity doesn't just cause us to ask questions; it also motivates us to form hypotheses or theories. When our expectations fail and we become curious about why they failed, we often test our explanations in the form of a hypothesis. For instance, many people's expectations about how government works failed during President Clinton's impeachment trial. Because they didn't understand it, they articulated hypotheses about it:

"It's all about politics."

"It's a moral catharsis."

"It's a secret conspiracy by Democrats to gain greater power because of the backlash against Republicans heading the witch-hunt."

When we're curious about any complex system such as this one, we not only float theories directly but tell each other stories that are indirect hypothesis testers: "This reminds me of the time when my sixth-grade teacher caught me copying someone else's answers and asked the class to vote on my punishment." It doesn't matter that our theories are wrong and that our stories don't provide illumination. By trading explanations in the form of stories and hypotheses, we're saying, "Here's my confusion about the world and my explanation for it." We're intensely interested in a complex subject and trying to get at the truth of it. None of this may look like inquisitiveness, but that's exactly what it is.

We want to preserve and foster this natural curiosity in our children. We want to put them in complex situations where their expectations fail and they ask questions and form hypotheses about things that interest them.

Translating Theory into Practice

Putting your child in situations where she can be inquisitive is something you need to do early. Once kids are in school, structured environments and rigid curriculums make it difficult for them to investigate their general interests. While you can implement the following approaches when your child is older, it's best if you start between the ages of three and five when they've moved past physical curiosity (playing with objects) to intellectual curiosity (playing with ideas):

1. Allow young children to express their curiosity even if it tries your patience.

This is trickier than it might seem. It's quite tempting to tell a toddler to stop exploring a room because you're afraid he'll break something. Your intentions may be good, but the results will be bad. While you don't want to endanger your child, you want to do everything possible to let his curiosity run wild. This means giving up your need for an orderly house where certain rooms are off limits and certain objects can't be touched. It may mean that your child breaks a few vases and bangs himself up a bit in his adventures, but at least his desire to explore and investigate will be fueled.

2. Expand the field of curiosity.

Curiosity is killed by scripts. If your child does the same thing day in and day out and never sees new places or people, he's not going to be as curious as he might otherwise be. Expanding the field means finding situations for your child that are a bit different, that challenge, confuse, and confound him. The things I've talked about previously—taking your child on trips, going to restaurants with unusual food—stimulate many of the traits of smarter kids. If your child lives in the suburbs, take him on outings to the city. If you're raising the quintessential city kid, take her camping. If your children live and breathe sports, take them to museums and concerts. A diverse group of experiences is a requisite for all six learning traits. Remember, even though your child is born curious, you need to give her as many things as you can to be curious about. Kids are especially curious about complex situations. For instance, adult arguments rivet a child's attention: he wants to know what the argument is about, why Daddy said that bad word, why Mommy is upset, and so on. Most parents shield their children from these arguments, believing that their kids are too sensitive to be exposed to the complicated and intense details of the argument. In reality, their curiosity should take precedence over their supposed sensitivities. Explain what the argument is about, and let them ask touchy questions and satisfy their curiosity.

3. Be there when your child is curious.

This is a simple requirement but one that parents in an increasingly time-strapped world have difficulty fulfilling. Your child needs to articulate his curiosity in order to develop it; it's not just having experiences that's important, but telling stories and floating hypotheses about those experiences. You need to be there to listen to your child's stories and theories and answer questions about the object of his curiosity.

To that end, it's wise to schedule simple activities with your child that provide an optimal environment for one-on-one conversation. Two easy things you can do is go for walks and take long bus rides. Like many teenagers, my daughter took a while before she was ready to express her curiosity. At the start of our walks and rides together, she wouldn't say much. By the end, she would be talking a mile a minute. You need activities that offer time and isolation: walking and riding the bus are two of the best.

4. Barely satisfy a child's curiosity.

As the old show business saying goes, "Leave them wanting more." Parents often overreact when their child is inquisitive about a subject; they tell their kids far more than they need or want to know. The child who begins asking questions about clouds receives a lecture that is every bit as boring and meaningless as a fact-filled lesson at school. All of us can absorb only so much—pile on too much information and we don't remember a thing. In most instances, what we want in response to our inquiries is one piece of information we can mull over.

You need to develop a sense about how much information your child wants. Sometimes this is as simple as seeing your child's eyes glaze over with boredom and recognizing he's had enough. To determine how to respond to a question, ask yourself why he's asking the question. If he just wants a simple fact—the name of a cloud formation—give him that and nothing more. If the motivation for the question is a deeper intellectual curiosity, say or do something that causes him to ask another question. For instance: "Let's go outside and look at the clouds and see what we can observe."

5. Ask your child questions about people, places, and things that really interest him.

Questions are a great way to stimulate your child's natural inquisitiveness but only if your question is about a subject that touches on a true interest. Many parents have a tendency to ask questions about what interests them or what is in their own areas of expertise. My son's curiosity was always intensified when I asked him questions about football—he loved the game. If I were to ask those same questions of my daughter, she would have absolutely no curiosity.

As I've emphasized earlier, it's also important that you not judge your child's interest as trivial, weird, or stupid, or fail to ask questions because a subject doesn't interest you or you know nothing about it. The least you can do is make an effort to learn something about his interest so you can ask intelligent questions. These questions will send him off exploring on his own; you'll open possible avenues of inquiry he may not have thought of before.

Kids can be jaded, bored, and lazy. They may have an interest but need a bit of a push to explore that interest. Your questions can provide that push. One of the biggest complaints of graduate students is expressed this way: "The problem with this field is that all the answers are known." In fact, there is plenty left to learn in most fields; they simply need to ask the questions from a different perspective. What professors do—and what you can do—is ask the questions that get them curious about a new way of looking at their field of interest.

Curiosity is easily stifled by unknowing parents. Perhaps the most insidious instance is when kids are made to feel stupid for being curious. "You wouldn't understand the answer" and "Ask me again when you're grown up" are two common responses. Almost as devastating is directly or indirectly communicating that you don't have time for your child's inquisitiveness. Responding to an inquiry by telling him to come back later when you're not busy (talking on the phone, doing work, watching television) devalues a child's curiosity.

Parents like this are involved in a covert conspiracy with schools to discourage inquisitiveness. Children are trained from the earliest grades to direct their questions to the point of the discussion rather than go off on their own. A teacher may be teaching kids to memorize the geographical location of European countries when a student remembers that throughout history these countries have had numerous wars with each other. He may wonder if the geographical proximity has a relationship to the frequency of wars fought over the years. Instead of engaging his interest by pursuing this line of thinking, most teachers will stifle discussion to move the original lesson along. Over time, students resist the urge to express real curiosity in class except on those rare occasions when it relates to the subject being taught.

To avoid being part of the educational system's conspiracy against curiosity, adopt the five techniques presented here.

Surface and Deep Curiosity

While all curiosity is good, curiosity that burrows into a subject is best. Some people are inquisitive only about surfaces; they're dilettantes, never investigating an area in any depth. From a practical standpoint, this won't get your child anywhere (except perhaps on game shows, where memorization of trivia is the goal). To become expert at anything, you need to be seriously curious; you can't be satisfied with simple answers to your questions or posit one theory about why something happens and accept the results as remaining true forever.

As I've emphasized before, one of the best ways to raise

smarter kids is by modeling smarter behavior. Here this is an especially apt concept. If you show your children that you refuse to accept simple answers—that you're going to get to the bottom of things—then they will imitate your deeply inquisitive ways.

When my children were growing up, they saw this in action. Once, when we were on a plane, the stewardess gave the usual warning about putting the seat back before takeoff. I asked her why we had to do this. "It's safer for you," she said. This didn't make sense to me. What would happen in a plane crash if the seat were not in a perfectly upright position? I kept on probing and eventually discovered that the airline wants the seats up so that other passengers can get out more easily in an emergency. The point is that my children observed me working hard to satisfy my curiosity and that I didn't automatically accept the first answer as the only one.

Understand that you're teaching your children to act in ways that aren't always socially acceptable; not accepting answers people give you can be a bit obnoxious. Deeply curious people are also somewhat rebellious. Still, it seems like a fair trade to exchange some social acceptability for being able to investigate a subject in depth.

Permissiveness Is Permitted

What all this comes down to is allowing your children to be curious about everything. This means lifting all the traditional restrictions parents place on kids—no drinking, no smoking, no sex, no drugs, no staying out late, no going to this party or listening to that type of music. You may find this difficult to do. It's scary to allow children to experiment.

But all this doesn't mean that you're advocating teen sex, hard drugs, or other dangerous behaviors. What you are doing is giving your children blanket permission to experiment. It's possible that they'll get in trouble because of this permissiveness; it's more likely they'll get in trouble if you don't give them this type of permission. For instance, some cultures allow kids to sip wine at religious ceremonies and family gatherings. Though there's no overt endorsement of alcohol, it's also not viewed as forbidden fruit. Parents don't deliver fire-and-brimstone sermons against demon rum, nor do they punish their children for drinking. In addition, they are perfectly willing to drink in front of their children (usually in association with a meal or ceremony of some type). They don't feel the need to hide their drinking or do it out of the house at a bar. It's no coincidence that these cultures generally have low rates of alcoholism.

This is as opposed to other cultures where there are stern warnings and punishments associated with alcohol. Kids are lectured about the dangers of drinking and absolute prohibition is the rule. This isn't to say that parents in these cultures don't drink, only that they do it in private. It's not surprising that a much higher percentage of people in these cultures have problems with alcohol as young adults. Again, part of this is the behavior modeled by parents. Kids hear their parents telling them not to drink but realize that they're drinking heavily. Parental hypocrisy is a sure way to produce undesirable behavior in children.

Experimentation is often a self-regulating process. When I was in college, I engaged in petty thievery like stealing street signs. I did it because it was fun. But doing it made me think about right and wrong, and eventually I decided that the prevailing view on such activities made sense. I was used to making up my own rules, but sometimes, I realized, society's rules should be taken seriously. I told my children that if they wanted to smoke marijuana, that was fine, but they had to try it first with me. After that, they didn't show much of a desire to smoke dope. I know of a family whose son wanted to wear a dress to the first day of school. They allowed him to wear it, he was ridiculed by the other kids, and he never wore one again.

Part of this self-regulation involves the forbidden fruit syndrome—things aren't nearly as enticing when they're allowed. Part of it is that the experimental behaviors result in reactions that discourage further experiments along those lines.

The larger issue, however, is that even if permissiveness leads to some minor problems, they're worth it if your child becomes intensely inquisitive. Children should see life as a buffet and be encouraged to try anything that interests them. This philosophy helps children find their niche in the world and become an expert at their chosen profession. It's interesting to note that in modern times, very few highly religious people are great scientists. Religion of any sort stifles curiosity; catechism answers all the big questions. This doesn't mean that religious kids are dumb; it's just that if you raise your children as strict observers of whatever religion you practice, they're not going to have much interest in exploring new behaviors and asking difficult questions. Why should they when they're focused on following beliefs and doctrines unquestioningly?

The other advantage of encouraging children to have all sorts of new experiences is that you'll be able to communicate with them better. Parents who vigorously oppose children on issues tend to shut the door on communication. Even worse, they encourage their children not to bring up certain subjects or to lie about them. Helping your child be inquisitive means being available to answer their questions or to help them find their own answers. You can't do this if you've made certain topics off-limits.

We live in a highly restrictive society, and this applies not just to adolescent behaviors but to every aspect of our culture. Americans, especially, are conservative creatures (in a social rather than a political sense). When I took my father and other family members out for his ninety-first birthday, we decided to go to a Japanese restaurant. My father's sister was horrified: "You're going to make me eat raw fish! I wasn't raised that way." Her attitude is common in people many years younger than she. All people are inherently conservative about food: We don't eat things that are too close or too far away from us. As a result, we're unwilling to eat cats and dogs (too close) or lions and zebras (too far away). Like many restrictions we place on everything from our eating to our dating to our travel habits, these are purely arbitrary. Breaking arbitrary rules is an inherent feature of inquisitive kids.

As a parent who wants to raise a curious child, you need to encourage the breaking of arbitrary social restrictions. This doesn't mean pushing them to commit murder; it does mean getting them to try raw fish.

Curiosity and Careers

How does inquisitiveness translate into success in adult life? It translates in obvious and not-so-obvious ways, and it depends on the profession a child chooses. For instance, my mother took me on a business trip to Europe when I was twenty. As part of her bead-importing business, she needed to meet her exclusive source in Austria. In the source's office, my mother and the man were talking and I, being a curious young man, began examining the papers on this man's desk. While I was perusing the papers, I noticed order blanks from my mother's competitors. Later I informed my mother that her source was reneging on their deal, and she was able to confront him with this information and use it to her advantage.

It's obvious why scientists need to be curious, but what about a stockbroker? I certainly want my stockbroker to be curious about why stocks go up or down; I want him to have a theory of the case that he can apply to increase the odds that my stocks will go up more often than they go down. Entrepreneurs require theories about trends and markets to keep growing their businesses; they're curious about which new market will emerge next and what trend might impact sales of their products; they investigate, ask questions (sometimes in the form of formal research), and test-market to satisfy their curiosity and confirm or disprove their theories.

Not all professions require inquisitiveness for success. The stewardess who gave me a stock answer about why seats needed to be in the full upright position had little need for curiosity. Airline pilots, too, probably aren't well served by inquisitiveness. They need to follow procedures and do what the manual, the tower, and their instruments tell them to do (a pilot who is curious if he could make better time by flying through a thunderstorm rather than avoiding it is not the pilot I'd want).

But in general, children will benefit from their curiosity. People who make breakthroughs, develop new products and concepts, and find better ways of doing their job are all driven by an insatiable curiosity.

3

Intervention Tactics

11

An Intelligent Approach to Sports

YOU may be reluctant to follow my suggestion made in earlier chapters that kids should play sports. It's possible that the image of the "dumb jock" dissuades you or perhaps you're skeptical that having your kid hit a ball or throw a pass has anything to do with intelligence.

This is understandable. I know a number of very bright individuals who share these views and went out of their way to disparage sports when their children were growing up. While their kids often had high IQs, many of them were underachievers who as adults didn't excel in their chosen fields or simply had problems choosing a field. While sports might not have been the cause of this indecision and underachievement, it was a neglected tool, one that might have made their kids more intellectually resilient and resourceful.

If you want to raise smarter kids, you should find a way to help them incorporate sports into their lives. The following will give you some ideas about how and when to do so.

What Happens When a Kid Strikes Out, Misses a Game-Winning Shot, or Drops a Pass

Expectation failure, as I've emphasized, is a trigger for learning. I've also noted that all sports are filled with expectation failures. Let's look at this failure in some depth and see what impact it has on the developing child.

Schools don't like children to experience failure of any type. No teacher ever tells students, "I want you to take risks and try things that really challenge you and are more complex than what you're used to. I especially want those of you who are bright and accustomed to success to stretch and see what it's like to fail. It's fine if you flunk a test now and then, as long as you do so in an interesting or adventurous way." Instead, kids are pushed toward continuous success. The students who receive the best grades and most awards are those who do what is expected of them; they always show their work, choose traditional topics to write about, underline in yellow marker what the teacher tells them they'll be tested on, and commit these facts to memory. Consistent success yields honor rolls, scholarships, placement in special classes, awards ceremonies, and other positive reinforcement. Kids know that if they follow the rules and do what they're told, they'll achieve success. The unexpected rarely happens.

In sports, the situation is significantly different. Sports don't explicitly encourage failure, but it's implicitly expected in just about every athletic activity. Most major league baseball players hit below .300 and recognize that they will fail more than two-thirds of the time. Basketball players miss at least half their shots, and quarterbacks expect to throw incomplete passes. No one wins all his games and many teams lose as often as they win. Most athletes are still shocked and surprised when they make mistakes and lose; the streak shooter expects to hit shot after shot and can't believe it when the ball starts clanking off the front of the rim. If you've ever watched small children playing any of these sports, you'll see much more failure. Kids can't make one basket out of twenty shots and have trouble even hitting a pitched ball. You would think that they would grow frustrated and quit, but few kids do. Instead, they keep plugging away until they get better.

This is an interesting phenomenon. When children are starting out, they expect to miss. For a while, their expectations are confirmed. With practice and perseverance, however, one day they don't miss. They're surprised when they make good contact with the ball and they smack it over the shortstop's head. This is one early type of expectation failure common to sports; they expected to do poorly and they do well. As they start doing well—even when they're very talented athletes and do extremely well—they experience expectation failure again. This time, however, they lose to a team they were sure they could beat or they drop a fly ball like the one they've caught hundreds of times.

In each of these cases, expectation failure catalyzes questions and a need to explain what happened. A child may ask himself, a coach, or another kid, "Why did I miss that ball?" One explanation may be "Because I took my eye off it for a second because I was distracted by the runner on base." Thus, the child learns to keep his eye on the ball and practices doing so until he becomes proficient.

Kids learn something else from the sports-related expectation failures that they often don't learn from other types of failures. When a kid fails a test in school or has trouble writing a paper and doesn't turn it in on time, he doesn't have to face that failure head-on. He can make excuses ("I was coming down with a cold") and whine his way out of it ("I would have done better if I didn't have so much homework that night"). While some whining and excuse-making occurs with sports failures, more often than not kids accept and learn from their mistakes. Their teammates are impacted by their failures, and there's a need for them to perform well in the present. Witnesses and the immediacy of the experience cause children to face their mistakes and attempt to explain them. This is especially true in pickup games and other informal competitions where failure is rarely viewed in catastrophic terms. Many times, kids will respond to a friend's failure with a pat on the back and words of encouragement. All of this facilitates reflection and explanation in the wake of failure.

There's another one of our learning paradoxes at play here, the idea of a purely physical activity helping a kid to become smarter. It's true that the physical aspect of sports is largely a non-thinking activity. In the heat of the moment, you don't have time to reflect upon whether you should shoot or drive to the basket. Decision-making in sports relies on instincts sharpened by experience. Think too long about your swing and you'll mess it up; try to analyze a play before making it and your window for action will close. At the same time, however, it fosters cognitive activity after the play is over. When there is time to think—after the game, during practice, and so on—your mind dwells on whatever expectation failure occurred and begins explaining and ultimately learning from what took place. In this way, sports fine-tunes the mind.

The Result Is Resilience

Expectation failure in sports ultimately produces a more resilient kid. If you want your child to do well in life, you want him to be able to dust himself off when he gets knocked down and rejoin the battle. Sports confers this ability on children, and it does so in a variety of ways.

First, it demonstrates that you get lots of chances even after you fail. You don't get just a few at-bats or play a few games. No matter what sport you're playing, it's an activity that you do over and over again. Baseball players learn that no matter how terrible a batting slump is, they'll eventually hit themselves out of it. Tennis players realize that they can lose a set 6–0 and still come back and win the match. The message all sports communicate is this: If you hang in there, eventually you'll do better or win.

Second, it provides you with a reserve of stories to draw on when resilience is necessary. Just about every kid has at least one inspiring sports story in which he beat the odds and his own expectations. My single greatest sports moment occurred when I was in summer camp and we had been divided into teams as part of a camp Olympics. I was playing tennis in this competition, and my team received a certain number of points depending on how well I did. If the game was close, we would receive a reasonable number of points even if I lost. I was matched against the best tennis player in camp, and no one, including me, expected that I had a chance; I was not a particularly good tennis player. My teammates were urging me to put up a good fight and win a few games so the team would get some points. With my teammates cheering me on, I not only won a few games but won the match. How I did this (essentially, I used a Muhammad Ali–type strategy and psyched him out) is not as important as the fact that I experienced huge expectation failure and beat someone I had no business beating. Throughout my life whenever I feel like I don't have a chance of achieving an ambitious objective, this story comes to mind and motivates me to keep trying.

These stories don't necessarily have to involve a child's participation in a sport. My son, for instance, is a big New York Mets fan, as am I. In 1986, when he was eleven, I took him to the sixth game of the World Series at Shea Stadium. I was not particularly well off at the time and couldn't really afford the scalper's prices, but it seemed like it was worth the price for the experience. Unfortunately, in the top of the tenth inning the Boston Red Sox had scored two runs and looked as though they were going to win the game and the series. Even though things looked bleak as the Mets were getting ready to take their last at-bats, I quoted Yogi Berra's malapropism to my son: "It ain't over till it's over." Amazingly (an appropriate word to use in conjunction with that Mets team), they came back to win the game and then the series. Ever since then, when my son gets down about something and wants to quit, the memory of the Mets' unexpected comeback helps him be more resilient.

Third, sports fosters a "graceful failure" mentality. Women traditionally take losing harder than men, and I'm convinced it's because many of them didn't play sports as children. They're often devastated when they lose a long-time customer or when an expected deal doesn't work out. Rather than recovering quickly and working on a new deal, they become discouraged and sometimes even quit.

Thankfully, our society began encouraging girls to play sports in the eighties, and I've noticed that the younger women I work with often are just as resilient as men. The point is that expectation failure can have tremendously negative consequences for people if they haven't developed resilience. My uncle, a football coach, had a sign over his desk that read, "A winner never quits and a quitter never wins." The sentiment might be hackneyed but the message was right. You can't fall apart every time something doesn't work out. Kids need to learn how to maintain their equanimity when they fail, and sports provides them with a good way to learn this lesson.

How Sports Reinforce Smarter Kid Traits

In a variety of ways, sports foster gumption, inquisitiveness, verbal ability, creativity, analysis, and ambition. Some of this is obvious. When you begin to realize that losing a game isn't the end of the world, you develop the gumption to keep at it, recognizing that you'll eventually have an opportunity to win.

It promotes ambition because when you miss a shot or lose a game, you're motivated to practice harder and improve your skills to achieve more; you develop a goal—to beat Team X—and are driven to do so.

It stimulates creativity because when you keep trying to beat someone, when you think you've developed a way to do so and still fail, you're pushed to be more creative in your approach. I play racquetball against a guy with a killer shot up front, and for a while I just couldn't return it. Eventually, I came up with a tactic that allowed me to keep the ball farther back.

In terms of analysis, this trait is often triggered when you keep trying but fail to win against a better opponent. If you keep coming up with new strategies that don't work, eventually you're forced to do a better job of analyzing and planning, and this analysis usually pays off. In college, I was a member of a fraternity that played intramural football; we were a group of small, skinny "intellectuals" who always lost to a jock fraternity of boys much bigger than we. Finally, in the championship game, we came up with a clever game plan that allowed us to steal a win, and it helped all of us understand that David versus Goliath has a basis in fact.

Inquisitiveness is launched by sports failures because you become tremendously curious when your brilliant game plan doesn't work out.

Even verbal ability is facilitated by sports—trash-talking and other types of bantering with opponents helps you learn to think on your feet; this is often true when your opponent is better than you expected or you're not doing as well as you thought, and your only recourse is a good-natured insult or a clever comment.

Being able to analyze how to win and having the ambition to win are crucial traits in our society. Outside of sports, the politically correct attitude kids grow up with is that everyone is a winner; that it's somewhat gauche to devise a scheme that allows you to capitalize on another person's weakness; that it's avaricious to want to win desperately. Sports teach kids that there are winners and losers, and that if you want to win, analysis and ambition are two essential traits. In sports, you're always exploiting weaknesses to gain an edge; winning is a clear and unambiguous goal, and to achieve it you need to defeat someone else. This is the way much of life is, and it's a lesson sports teach well.

How to Help Kids Take Advantage of Sports

Pushing your child to play a sport you played, insisting he join the youth soccer league because everyone else in the neighborhood is joining, or signing your child up for tennis lessons isn't particularly useful if you want to raise a smarter kid. Although these are typical parental tactics, here are some atypical actions that will be of much greater help to your children:

1. Encourage "disorganized" rather than organized sports.

Certainly kids can derive some of the same benefits playing in organized leagues that they can from pickup games; it's just that the latter offers kids unique opportunities to learn that are often absent from more organized activities. For instance, in a pickup game kids have all sorts of opportunities for analysis, verbal jousting, and creativity that are missing from leagues and school sports. They can argue with one another about who should be on which team; they don't have to conform to a coach's rules, freeing them to be much more creative in their playing (making hot dog moves on the basketball court) and planning (devising highly creative football plays in the dirt).

Expectation failure is also more "tolerable" for kids in pickup games, and thus a better learning catalyst. In organized sports, children are much more anxious about how they do. In Little League, for instance, they're playing under the watchful and often critical eyes of parents and coaches. Any type of failure in this situation can be traumatic. Rather than learning from the failure and seeking explanations for it, they become uptight and unable to focus on their mistakes. Either they are made so miserable by the failure that they quit or they try and quickly correct a mistake out of fear of making it again (and therefore aren't motivated by a real goal that causes them to be curious about what happened and willing to be creative in exploring ways to do better the next time).

In short, pickup games are often more fun than organized sports, and fun creates a much more fertile environment for learning than fear. While organized sports can be beneficial if a child really enjoys the sport and finds it fun to play in a league or for his school, parents should push pickup games for most kids.

2. Let your child choose her sport rather than choosing the sport for her.

You probably know more than one parent who insisted a child do a particular sport because "it will be good for her" or because the parent loves the sport. Kids will find their own favorite sports if you leave them to their own devices. Most children will naturally play a variety of games with friends and eventually find one that suits their fancy. It doesn't matter if they choose an individual or a team sport, a popular one or a more esoteric endeavor. Whether they opt for fencing or football, they will learn from their experiences.

What you can do to encourage sports is play simple games of catch with your child, take her to play tennis with you, go in the backyard and kick a soccer ball around, and even invent running and catching games. It's also fine to watch different sports with your child, ideally at the event itself rather than on television. The goal here isn't to find a sport your child can excel at as much as one that she finds fun to play and compete in.

A learning bonus to informal sports play with children is that it's an ideal time for talking. Throwing a ball back and forth creates a relaxed, natural environment in which your child will feel free to ask you questions and listen to your answers. A bond is created through play that transcends sports and helps facilitate honest communication.

3. Keep your children away from tyrannical coaches.

People can praise successful dictator-type coaches all they want; I would strongly advise you to pull your child off any team coached by a ranting and raving, win-at-any-cost coach. These are often mean, rigid people who not only won't let your child fail gracefully, but will make it difficult for him to exhibit any creativity.

4. Encourage your child to play sports even if he isn't a natural athlete.

Sports are beneficial even for geeks, dorks, and dweebs. Unless children are so uncoordinated that they're a danger to themselves, they can reap benefits by playing pickup games with other kids. They may have to endure being picked last for teams, playing right field, and the like, but they'll eventually be accepted by other kids if they stay with it. Expectation failure occurs when, to everyone's surprise, they get a hit or catch a pass when it counts. This event prompts them to explain why this happened. When they hit upon an explanation, it doesn't necessarily help them become much better at a given sport—they are limited by a lack of natural physical ability—but it does help them learn important lessons about success. They discover that if they stick with a sport long enough—if they display a certain amount of gumption—it will pay off. They find that if they're more creative about their approach to the game—if they run a new pass route or change their swing—they do better.

This type of learning is difficult to come by for many geeks, dorks, and dweebs. Typically, the very bright, unathletic kid sticks to his natural area of excellence and never has the diverse experiences sports offer. Not only doesn't he have the range of experience that facilitates learning but he has relatively little expectation failure in his life—he sticks with what he excels at and his expectations are consistently met.

For me, math was easy; I could do it my sleep and rarely encountered problems that I couldn't solve. But when I ventured into the world of sports, I had many expectation failures, not only in sports like tennis that I wasn't good at, but sports like football or baseball, where I had some talent. My most important sports memory is about the sport I was worst at. I won lots of football games, but they never had the impact on me that that one tennis match had because I was no damn good at tennis.

5. Give them opportunities to talk about their sports experiences.

This gives kids a chance to test their hypotheses and figure out why they failed. Remember, stories aren't just stories; they're ways of testing theories about expectation failure and asking for responses to these theories. Listen to anyone tell a sports-related story, and more often than not it has to do with expectation failure and involves a possible explanation for that failure. When people are participants in sports, they talk about how they made an impossible shot (that they didn't expect to make), how they beat a superior team (that they didn't expect to beat) or lost to an inferior team (that they expected to beat). When they're observers, they recall how a favorite team won when they were expected to lose or vice versa. These stories are always accompanied by some form of explanation, either explicit or implicit—we lost because our star player was injured; I played well because I visualized how I would hit a home run in a crucial situation.

Therefore, ask your children how the pickup basketball game went or if their intramural team did well. Become involved as a coach or as an observer if your child is participating in an organized sport so you can ask more informed questions—questions that better elicit stories. Just knowing your child's fears and talents related to a particular sport—and being aware of the other children your child plays sports with and his feelings about them as athletes—can help you ask questions that stimulate him to tell stories.

One of the Few Adult Experiences Children Can Have

Younger children live in a fantasy world. Much of what goes on in their lives bears little relationship to what takes place in the world of adults. Most kids have little responsibility or accountability. By the time they are of school age, they enter into an equally unreal environment where goals are artificial and meaningless (no one is born with an innate desire to get an A in social studies) and success is measured by doing what one is told and avoiding failure.

It's important to give children a chance to experience the real world, and sports offers that chance. The expectation failure, the competition, the meaningful goals that motivate people to do better—all these are important. If you doubt this, ask any adult (preferably a man since many women were denied the opportunity to participate in sports) about his most salient childhood memories. It's likely that he'll tell you a sports-related story. I was in an arts and crafts class when I was nine at summer camp when a counselor in charge of the older boys interrupted the class to say that their pitcher had hurt himself in an inter-camp game. He wanted me to leave class at once and take this pitcher's place. Being chosen to pitch against boys two and three years older than I in a big game provided me with a memorable experience. It nurtured a sense of self-worth and ambition that no other childhood activity was capable of nurturing.

I didn't become a great baseball pitcher, but I was never afraid to take on problems that seemed above my abilities.

12

School Interventions

PARENTS are constantly asking me "what if" and "what should I do" questions related to school. They range from concerns about nursery school to problems with graduate school and include inquiries such as: "Is private school better than public school for my child?" "What should I do if my child hates his teacher?" "Should I tolerate my daughter getting B's?" "What college is best for my son?"

As a result of the schools' antipathy toward failure, obsession with teaching to the test, reliance on a highly standardized and structured curriculum, and other factors, these questions can be confusing for parents. They're especially confusing if you answer them the way the schools want them answered, relying on the misconceptions and misinformation they perpetuate. You feel like you're making the right decisions for your child, but your child feels bored, stupid, and miserable. Chapter 2 as well as other chapters were written to correct some of the more egregious myths manufactured by the educational system.

Still, if you're like most parents, you'll want to know *what to do* in a wide variety of situations. In the course of your child's school career, he'll face hundreds of situations that will bother and bewilder both of you. I know parents who have spent months just trying to figure out whether to send their child to a public or a private high school. My goal here is to help you figure out when and how to intervene. I've identified the most common questions parents ask related to school, and the following should give you some ideas about what to do when you're faced with them.

Which Nursery School Should My Child Go To?

It's astonishing how many parents agonize over what is essentially a trivial issue. Whether your kid goes to the most expensive, exclusive nursery school in your area or the place where the poorest people in your community send their children, the net effect will be the same from a learning standpoint. That's because nursery school is about parents and play and not about learning and kids. What goes on in nursery school is a lot of running around, coloring, and listening to stories. This is fine for socialization purposes and kids may enjoy themselves, but they certainly don't gain a head start or any type of competitive edge. Nursery schools are really there for stay-at-home parents who are going out of their minds because they're spending every waking second with their children, or for working moms who need day care. Because our society doesn't have communal child-raising and the extended family often isn't around to share in this task, parents need a break; it's difficult to be a good parent without one.

Just about everything taught in nursery school can be learned by a child in other and better ways. The six smarter kid traits aren't brought out by nursery school, and in fact some anti–smart kid traits such as learning how to sit quietly and to follow orders unquestioningly are sometimes instilled. There are, of course, some innovative nursery schools that may do a better job than others in allowing a child to explore his interests— they're not under the thumb of a bureaucratic school administration, after all. Unfortunately, many of these schools don't take advantage of this freedom. If you can find one that does, it might be worth signing your child up.

Still, you can do something far more important during these preschool years than any nursery school can: *Teach your child to read.* Doing so early will increase the odds that your child will view reading as a pleasurable activity. In school, reading is taught as a group activity; everyone reads the same stupid book at the same slow speed. It's difficult to turn reading into a chore, but school manages to do just this. If you teach your child one-on-one, you can make it fun. Not only can you move at your child's natural speed, but you can choose books that specifically interest her.

What Should I Do If My Child's Teacher Is Making Her Miserable?

School is hell for children whose teachers pick on them or treat them poorly in some way. School is tolerable when teachers treat them fairly or actually demonstrate a liking for them. Parents have a remarkable degree of control over the child-teacher relationship, though many of them don't realize the power they have or are unwilling to use it.

For many years, parents assumed that teachers knew best. No matter what a child's complaints about a teacher might have been, the child was assumed to be in the wrong. Parents held teachers in high regard, much like doctors. Many people would not even protest if a teacher hit their child, figuring that the kid provoked the teacher and that the discipline was good for him.

Today, most parents recognize that teachers (like doctors) are fallible and need to be held accountable. They understand that their child's teacher may lack both experience and skill; that she may even be a little tyrant who has come to despise both her profession and the children she's responsible for. I have empathy for teachers who are tough-minded and discipline-oriented—I would be the last person to underestimate the difficulty of controlling a classroom of thirty children, some of whom can be extremely irritating and needy. Nonetheless, this is no excuse for crossing the line and treating children savagely or sadistically.

If your child is clearly terrified of a teacher or talks about how a teacher makes him feel dumb or ostracized in any way, you should take action. If a teacher robs your child of self-esteem at an early age, that teacher decreases the odds of your child developing the traits described in this book. This teacher will make your child fearful of pursuing a creative idea or demonstrating gumption.

Here are some things you can do proactively and reactively to prevent a teacher from making school a more negative experience than it has to be:

1. Establish a relationship with the teacher.

Children who get picked on the most are the ones whose parents have no contact with the teachers. If you talk to your child's teacher—if you let her know who your child is, what her interests are, what her worries are—then the teacher will probably have a much better relationship with your child. If you establish a level of respect and communication with the teacher—if she understands you're an intelligent, caring parent—this will also help. Most teachers aren't evil. Many times, they don't realize they've made your kid feel worthless or incompetent. Once they really get to know both you and your child, they'll usually treat your child reasonably well.

2. Confront or intimidate the teacher.

While teachers usually aren't evil, some are angry and unhappy and take it out on their students. If for some reason your child gets their dander up, you are your child's best line of defense. When teachers responded in this manner to my children, I went to school and confronted them. Granted, as an expert in learning science I was able to bully them from a position of authority. But all you need to do is meet with the teachers and make it clear you're unhappy with their attitude and behavior and that you're going to be keeping close tabs on how they deal with your child. Usually, this is enough to get them to lay off.

3. Pull your kid out of a class taught by a truly awful teacher.

When a teacher, a former marine, intimidated my child with his drill instructor tactics, I simply told my son to go to the library and read science books. The first day he did this, the librarian asked him what he was doing there, and he replied that I had told him he was not allowed to go back to science class. The school readily went along with my plan. They recognized that they had a bad teacher on their hands and that my solution was probably the best for all concerned. They certainly didn't want me confronting this teacher and making numerous visits to the principal's office. It's very difficult to run a school, and the last thing a principal wants is a parent who makes it even more difficult. In elementary and even middle school, kids can easily get away with not taking one class. As long as the school feels they're learning the subject—on their own or with the help of a parent or tutor—it's usually satisfied.

I'm not saying you should routinely pull your kid out of class. Socially, this isn't easy on the kid who is pulled. But if a teacher is torturing your son or daughter, you may need to resort to this tactic. It may seem a little crazy, but schools have great respect for parents who act a little crazy—the last thing they want is a nutty parent filing a lawsuit or circulating a petition among other parents for a teacher's removal.

Can I Take My Child Out of School for Days, Weeks, or Months?

People ask this question fearing either that the school will punish their child for being absent or that they will somehow do irreparable harm to their kid by keeping him out of school. In terms of the latter concern, it's more likely that irreparable harm will be done by leaving him in school. In terms of the former issue, one of the big misconceptions parents labor under is that every day of school is sacrosanct and that it is some sort of secular sin to keep a child out of school when she isn't ill. Punishment, it is assumed, will be swift and certain.

The truth is that you can take your child out of elementary and middle school without repercussions. Oh, the school may grouse a bit, and your child will have to make up the work she missed. But the reality is, if your child is reasonably bright she'll be able to make up the work relatively quickly. In the lower grades, teachers move at a snail's pace, a pace set by the slowest learners. In third-grade math, you spend the first month or two reviewing everything you learned in second-grade math. Books are read equally slowly. Every course takes five times as long to teach as it should. As a result, children can make up a few weeks of missed school in a few days. At worst, your son or daughter might have to attend summer school to compensate for an absence that goes beyond a few weeks. By high school, it's more difficult to take children out of school because of course credits and prerequisites—they need to successfully complete a specific course to receive credit and so they can take the next required course in the series. Even then, however, many kids can do enough studying on their own to pass high school tests that are often the only (or the most significant) factor determining whether they pass or fail.

I'm not suggesting removing kids from schools just because you can. Obviously this is something parents should do with discrimination, recognizing the impact missing school might have on their child; it probably is a good idea to talk to your child about what he's going to be missing when you take him out and whether it's something he doesn't want to miss (or if it will result in homework that will be difficult to make up). The goal of an out-of-school experience is the learning that will take place.

Specifically, look for experiences that will bring out smarter kid traits. Perhaps the most common opportunity is taking a trip somewhere. When my children were in school, I took them with me all the time, and they missed big chunks of school without suffering any negative consequences. In fact, my daughter spent a large part of kindergarten in Barbados and much of ninth grade in France. What they gained—and what you can give your children—is a surefire way to catalyze the learning process. As I've emphasized, taking your child on trips is a great way to diversify their experiences, ensure expectation failure, and encourage them to talk about that failure. If I were in charge of the schools, I would make a one-week trip with a parent a prerequisite for being promoted to the next grade. It doesn't have to be a trip to anywhere exotic; it just has to be to a place the child has never been where she can experience new situations.

Should I Send My Child to a Public, Private, or Specialized School?

The answer to this question depends on the type of child you have. Typically, parents view private schools as more of a "fix" to a child's problems than they actually are. Realistically, you can expect a private school to provide your child with more personal attention because of the smaller class size. You'll also find that the teachers—especially in the humanities—tend to be more knowledgeable about their subjects. Private schools also offer teachers more freedom to be original in their teaching methods. In short, private schools tend to be more fun for kids and somewhat more tailored to who they are as individuals. But they're not panaceas. They still resemble public schools with their emphasis on grades, teaching to the test, and standardized curriculums. If your child is truly miserable at a public school, private school might be an option worth considering, but the responsibility for raising a smarter child is still much more in your hands than in the school's.

Because of the expense of private schools, you might also want to investigate whether your public school has special "smart kid" programs. While they're run under different names—honors, talented and gifted, advanced placement—they frequently provide the same individual attention as private schools and also take a more accelerated approach to various subjects.

Specialized schools have proliferated in recent years. They focus their coursework on everything from music to drama to math and science to the arts. There's even a school in New York for students who want aviation careers, and "trade" schools of various types exist throughout the country. For students who can find the right match between their interest and the school's focus, these schools may be a good choice. If they're absolutely certain that this is the subject they love and they're good at it, a specialized school can help them develop a sense of self and make them feel special. They're not a good choice, however, if kids are pipe-dreaming: the fourteen-year-old student who thinks it would be neat to be a famous actress, for instance. As you know, many teenagers have completely unrealistic career dreams, and they may be better served by a school that gives them a wider range of experiences via extracurricular activities as well as courses. Some kids need to explore different areas of interest before they find the one that makes sense for them.

In considering which school is right for your child, understand that the wrong choice is one that forces your child to move out of the house and away from you. Children become smarter in large part because of their parents' presence. You're the one to whom they most want to ask their inquisitive questions; you're the one whose approval they seek for their creative ideas. If you're not physically there and interacting with them on a daily basis, who is going to take your place? Even a great teacher or a best friend is not an adequate substitute. Send your child to boarding school and you're sending him away from the one person (or two people) who will always be his best teacher.

Keeping your children at home increases the odds that they'll maintain the emotional health necessary to become smarter kids. Kids who live away from home often develop values that aren't conducive to pursuing an interest; they aren't motivated to ask questions or place themselves in diverse situations where they risk failure. The presence of a parent provides the stability necessary to take risks and ask tough questions.

My Child Complains That School Is Boring; How Can I Get Him to Be More Interested in His Schoolwork?

You can't force him to become interested in something that he really does believe is boring. You'll get nowhere insisting that he "work harder," providing negative or positive sanctions or giving him a lecture about how he doesn't know what will be important later in life, so he should try to do well at everything. What you can do is set up a parallel school universe in which you're the only teacher and your child is the only student. In your school system, however, the goal isn't to get good grades but to experience expectation failure.

You can do this in a variety of ways. Let's say your kid comes home with a dull-as-dirt social studies assignment to write a paper on the exports of South America. Push your child to do the assignment in an interesting way. Let's say your child loves music. Suggest that he include music as an export; get some Tito Puente compact discs and play them at home; have your child estimate how much in tourism dollars this music might produce; ask him if music is more important to Latin America or North America as an export.

You can do this with any assignment. When your fourth grader comes home with the prototypical assignment to write about what he did on his summer vacation, start a dialog with him about what makes summer vacations interesting: where would he like to go next year and why; where would he like to go if no parents were allowed and he could travel with his friends?

When my children were taking math classes, I used to ask them to do their homework in odd ways. At first they protested that "we don't have to know this for the test," but I convinced them that they needed to know it for *my* test. They passed only if they showed some creativity about a subject, if they verbalized an idea related to it, if they analyzed it in a compelling way, and so on. Sometimes you only need to ask them a Socratic question or two in order to get their minds moving in a direction that interests them. Once you see that they're being more creative in their approach or ambitious in their choice of topic, you've done your job. Certainly you want to avoid giving them a lot more work than they already have, but you do want to help them find an angle to an assignment that intrigues them.

When I was a child I remember bringing home a 90 on a history test, a rare accomplishment for me (I wasn't particularly good in this area). I proudly displayed the test for my father, who gave it a disdainful glance and said, "You don't know anything about history." Though his method was wrong, his point was right. My ability to memorize facts about history had nothing to do with real knowledge of the subject, of why wars are fought and the egos and desire for power that shape eras. My father knew something about this subject, and if he were so inclined, he could have asked me questions that would have encouraged me to start digging on my own, to look at history from a personal standpoint (why did my grandfather leave the old country and settle in New York rather than Montana?).

What Should I Do About My Child's Average Grades?

It depends on what you mean when you say average. Grade inflation has made it difficult to earn less than a C in most classes—just showing up will usually guarantee that "average" grade. If a child receives a D, it means that he failed to show up and he managed to anger the teacher in some way.

Therefore, if your child is receiving C's and D's, you should be concerned. If your child is reasonably bright, these grades are unacceptable. They signify that he's just goofing off, and that's not behavior you want to condone. Even when he finds his area of interest and loves his job, there will be tasks within it that are mundane or irksome. He has to exhibit a certain amount of gumption to stick with a task and get it done; he needs to be sufficiently ambitious to do this task in order to achieve a more important goal. Communicating that laziness is acceptable behavior is not a good lesson to impart.

At the same time, you don't want to turn your child into a grade grubber or make her feel guilty for receiving B's instead of A's. The difference between a B and an A is negligible—both signify effort, and that's all you should ask for. In fact, some C's are acceptable if your child excels in her areas of interest.

As I've noted, my son and daughter told me it was hard being my children because I said grades didn't matter but I yelled at them when they received bad grades. In the paradoxical world of education, this is exactly the attitude I recommend. This will prevent your child from inculcating goofing off as a trait and will also reduce the stress that straight A students place on themselves.

If your child is receiving poor grades, you need to:

- **Clearly communicate that this behavior is unacceptable.** Your approval is critical to him (though it might not always seem that way), and therefore you need to get this across.
- **Help him become more interested in his schoolwork.** This might entail previous suggestions related to becoming his teacher at home and giving him more engaging and challenging assignments. It might also involve encouraging him to get better grades in the subjects he loves and simply put in some effort to receive modest grades in the subjects that are of less interest.

If your child is obsessed with receiving top grades, you need to:

- **Demonstrate that you really don't care if he receives A's or B's or even some C's.** This is difficult for some parents who reflexively rejoice when their child is named to the honor roll or fondly reminisce about how they were the valedictorian of their class. It means shrugging off a C or B and not pushing the child to work harder for the sake of working harder. Every time I see one of those bumper stickers that advertises that someone's kid is an honor roll student, I cringe. Parents need to be proud of their kid's love of learning, not their grade-point averages.
- **Encourage nonacademic activities that are fun for your child.** You want your child to work hard and do well at something, even if it has nothing to do with school subjects. Whether it's a photography club, building model airplanes, or making home movies, you want him to learn the importance of having fun. It also helps if you as the parent model this behavior; that instead of being a workaholic you take time off to pursue a hobby you love.

You might also want to relate the following story to your straight A student. I was attending my son's graduation from college, and one of the speakers was the class valedictorian. She started out by explaining how she had worked very hard to receive the best grades and refused to settle for anything less than an A. Then she said all this effort and stress "was a complete waste of time. I didn't come away with a love of learning, and looking back, I'm sorry that I did what I did." The audience was shocked and chagrined, but I felt like cheering. What a great lesson for these young people to receive. Talk about expectation failure; no one there was going to forget this particular experience.

It's also important to understand that for most kids, grades don't matter in terms of academic or career achievement. While it's true that colleges and graduate schools consider grades in admission decisions, they also consider other factors such as test scores and extracurricular activities. More significantly, your child can get into a good school without top grades. When parents complain to me that their children don't have the grades to get into Harvard or Yale, I suggest they send them to the University of Maryland or the University of Texas, which are perfectly fine schools (and there are a variety of other state schools that are quite good). In addition, your child can get into good graduate schools in a wide variety of subjects without top grades. If they want to go to the top law, medical, and business graduate schools, they do need superior grades because the competition is so fierce. There really are many interesting professions other than these three, and furthermore, these aren't always great choices. Few fields have more dropouts than law—large numbers of very bright kids become disillusioned with the law, finding it boring and unrewarding. Doctors are under tremendous stress these days, accounting for the high alcohol and drug dependency rate in the medical profession. And MBAs are a dime a dozen, with some major corporations moving away from hiring them and toward people with more diverse liberal arts backgrounds. What I'm implying is that your smarter kid may be better off just getting decent grades and avoiding the few professions that demand top grades.

Here's a truism to keep in mind when you're looking over your child's report card:

It's much easier to recover from bad grades than from good ones.

There are lots of second chances in academic life. Talk to twenty high-achieving people, and at least half of them will tell you that they received average or slightly above average grades for years until they found what really interested them and were motivated to do better. My grade point average in college was a little bit better than a C. And even if you receive mediocre grades in college and graduate school, employers don't care. I'm always telling my graduate students that they don't need straight A's to get jobs as assistant professors; that after they receive a Ph.D., no one wants to see their transcripts; that the important things are what they've published and what their professors say about them.

Good grades, however, are much more difficult to recover from. For one thing, kids who have killed themselves for A's have trained themselves to submit to a teacher's will and rarely if ever challenge an accepted opinion or posit a revolutionary idea. They are conditioned to be compliant, and compliance is not a trait of smarter kids. They are also conditioned to receive institutional praise, and as a result have difficulty transitioning to the world of work, where praise is often hard to come by. Many straight A students find that their bosses expect them to do well and don't compliment them every time they complete an assignment; that a learning curve in the working world can take months or years to climb, and that failure is more often the norm than success. For young adults accustomed to years of unbroken "perfection," the obstacles and frustrations of any new job are difficult to swallow.

How Can I Help My Child Choose the Right College?

You can help him by disabusing him of all the weird and nonsensical ideas he has about where he should go to college. Here are some of the wrongheaded notions that prompt kids (as well as parents and high school counselors) to choose the wrong schools:

1. One of my parents is an alumnus.
2. When I visited, the other kids seemed nice.
3. It's small, and I want to go to a small school (or it's big, and I want to go to a big school).
4. They've got a great football team.
5. The girls (or boys) are really good-looking.
6. The campus is beautiful.
7. It feels like a warm and friendly place.

In this country, there are perhaps fifty good, large research-oriented universities and about twenty-five solid, smaller liberal arts colleges. Beyond that, you're taking your chances, and you're likely to end up with second-rate professors and a limited selection of classes. The ratings in places like *U.S. News and World Report* are reasonably reliable, so use their rankings as a guide in helping your child choose a school. They will indicate the schools that have the best professors and the widest selection of classes. This combination will make it more likely that a student will find an interest that truly captivates him and a teacher who can push and challenge him.

One of the most pervasive misconceptions is that a small liberal arts college always provides a better education than a big research university. While it's true that a smaller school may offer smaller class sizes and more personal attention from a professor, what they lack is all the subject variations and unusual and esoteric disciplines found in a larger school. At the major research universities, you'll find classes in everything from the human genome to artificial intelligence; you'll find professors blazing trails in all sorts of emerging fields. This is important when viewed within our smarter kid framework. Many students end up being doctors, lawyers, or businesspeople by default; they're not exposed to the multiplicity of subjects out there, they lack the diverse experiences necessary for expectation failure to take place, and their curiosity about this failed area isn't piqued. As a result, highly intelligent students fall into the "standard" careers for bright kids: they go to law, medical, or business school; start working; and discover that they made a big mistake. There's this notion in our society that if you're really smart, you should pursue one of these three careers. For some people, this is fine. But if you are brainwashed into believing these are your only three career possibilities, you may overlook a job that you're passionate about in favor of one that's "acceptable."

As a parent, you want to expose your smart kid to various career possibilities, especially if she hasn't found a prospective career or interest that she's passionate about. Large universities provide the best exposure to diverse academic experiences and teachers with all sorts of new and interesting ideas. These universities have the money and research facilities necessary to attract these teachers. If your child is dead-set on becoming an English professor, a small, out-of-the-way school may be fine. Smaller schools often attract good professors in the humanities; they just don't provide the wide range of opportunities outside of this area.

How Can I Help My College-Aged Child Find Her True Calling?

Here are the words of wisdom you can impart to your child as she departs for college:

Follow the course of least resistance intellectually and most resistance politically.

"Least resistance intellectually" means doing what comes easier for you than others. For instance, I find it very easy to design software while others struggle mightily at this task. Because this skill comes naturally, it makes sense that it would be something that I would turn into a career. Many children and their parents, however, believe that there's something noble about struggle. I know people who deliberately avoid what comes easily because "there's no challenge." Choosing a career because you want to become good at something that's difficult is a masochistic game. Just because you find something easy doesn't mean you can't find challenges in that arena; you just have to take risks and create complex and puzzling assignments for yourself.

"Most resistance politically" means charting a course where the world doesn't want you to go. When I was in college and decided to teach computers to understand English, I met with a great deal of resistance from traditionalists in linguistics. But this resistance demonstrated that there were opportunities to explore new subjects and propose fresh ideas. I made inroads in my field faster than other young graduate students because I had found my niche. Or more appropriately, I was carving out a new niche that I could make my own. When experts in a given field warn you off some area of study, your antennae should start quivering. Most experts are traditionalists, and you're not going to make much progress (or make it quickly) following the same path as the rest of your colleagues. In any field, you'll progress further and faster if you develop your own area of expertise. In addition, encountering resistance is good for your intellectual development. When you present what you feel is a great new idea to a traditional boss and he shoots it down, you experience expectation failure. This failure provides the impetus to begin investigating why the idea failed and refining it to make it stronger (or coming up with an even better idea). This process is fun; it's exciting to go up against the norm; it's energizing to marshal arguments in favor of your idea. Going with the political flow is boring. Going against it revs up your mind and gets you thinking.

But this general advice may not suffice. Your college student may be overwhelmed with all the choices college presents or underwhelmed by his lack of interest in any particular academic subject. Your child may not be one of the lucky ones who has discovered an area that turns him on and that he wants to somehow turn into a career; the lucky ones have at least a general idea about what to major in and where to apply for jobs or to graduate school in order to pursue their interests. If your child appears lost and confused about what to study in college, here are some things you might do.

First, advise your child that if he doesn't find a major that interests him, he should talk with his counselor or a professor about designing a major tailored to his interests. A relatively little known fact about college is that majors aren't always prescribed; many schools (especially private universities) are open to ideas about creating new majors and flexible about designing a set of requirements.

But let's say your child's school won't do this or your child doesn't know what type of major to design. Explain to him that majors really don't matter that much. A psychology degree will not give him a license to practice psychology. The key is to find courses that are fun and interesting. When my son asked for advice about what to major in, I suggested (not altogether facetiously) that he major in subways because that's what fascinated him. (He took my advice seriously and majored in urban studies, whatever that is.)

Still, some kids will struggle. They may find it difficult to recognize or acknowledge what their interests are. My daughter is now doing Web design, but for years she avoided computers (in part because they were too closely aligned with my field).

If your child tells you or demonstrates that she has no interest in being in school, suggest that she drop out. It's a far better experience for her to be out in the world exploring different jobs than stuck at a place in which she has zero motivation to learn. Many young people have a very narrow band of experience, most of which has been dominated by school. Exchanging the school environment for the working world can produce a wide range of new experiences, one of which may lead to an interest or a career. It also is useful for these dropouts to spend a lot of time in bookstores and libraries. What a young person chooses to read often provides insights into a future field of study or a career. In school, the reading requirements are so structured that it's difficult to find these clues. When people have complete freedom of reading choice, however, they often sample all types of books and find some subject that mesmerizes them. This subject might guide their choice of study should they return to college.

If you're at all concerned about telling your child to drop out of college, you may be interested to know that students who come back after being in the workforce for a few years are much more committed to their studies and much less interested in getting drunk and going to parties. These are the kids who are in school for the right reasons, and they're motivated to learn what is being taught and using it to explore career possibilities. One big problem with college is that it really isn't for the young. It's discouraging how many students view college as a social experience rather than a place to learn. Allowing your child to drop out of school may be the best way to put him on the path to learning at some point in the future.

13

The Myths and Realities of Computer-Based Learning

MANY parents labor under harmful misconceptions about the role computers play in their child's education. People are convinced that if they buy their child a computer and some of the most popular "educational software" titles and send him to special classes to learn computer skills, they will have given him an intellectual edge. In reality, all of this will have about the same effect as buying their child the latest shoot-'em-up software game. Both computers and games may be fun to play, but they're not set up for real learning experiences. Nonetheless, parents as well as the schools view computers as an educational panacea, believing that teaching a child to use a computer, to send e-mail to his friends, to create his own Web site, or to play with educational software will enrich his mind.

The value of computers depends exclusively on what's on the screen, and unfortunately a lot of what's on the screen is worthless. That's the bad news. The good news is that in theory, computers are the answer to our prayers for a better educational system. Or rather, they're the ideal educational tool for implementing some of the learning theories mentioned here. Computers are potentially capable of helping students develop the six traits of smarter kids. Before discussing what you can do to help your child capitalize on computers, let's look at why their potential has gone largely untapped.

Natural Learning, Unnatural Development

One-on-one instruction involving a parent and a child is as natural to animals as it is to people. A mother elephant shows her baby how to pick up things with his trunk; he learns by trying, failing, and practicing, and eventually he gets it right. This natural model is antithetical to a teacher standing up in front of thirty students and lecturing. Computers, however, provide an alternative for schools that's more like the mother elephant and her baby. Ideally, every student would spend part of the day at the computer working on software of his choice. Perhaps there would be a thousand different programs available, each geared toward a different interest. Some might involve academic subjects, others would be more technical in nature, and still others would focus on specific skills. Each program would simulate a real-life situation, allowing students to make decisions, confront people, solve problems, and so on. When the student would become stuck, he would be able to call on an expert who would be part of the simulation to answer questions or provide suggestions. For instance, one simulation might be about running a business. The student would assume the role of a store owner,

making purchasing decisions, dealing with complaining cus-
tomers, and so on. Each simulation would challenge the student
to solve a problem or deal with a situation he found meaningful.

This type of computer simulation would dovetail with natural
learning principles. The student would be learning by doing
rather than by passively listening; he would be motivated to
achieve the goal set up by the simulation; he would experience a
number of expectation failures but not be embarrassed by them
or afraid to fail because these failures would occur in private; and
he would learn on his own and with the help of an expert.

Computer simulations such as this aren't a futuristic dream.
They exist today, though the simulation most people are familiar
with involves the air flight simulator used to teach pilots to fly.
While they are expensive to produce, computer simulations aren't
widely available for reasons besides cost. Cost analysis would
demonstrate that the long-term gain in knowledge and expertise
would far offset the investment in software. The obstacles to making these simulations widely available in schools and to parents at
home are more complex. Rather than get into all the reasons—a
long discussion that is somewhat tangential to the purpose of this
book—let's just examine what happened in the eighties when
the schools began purchasing personal computers.

At that time, textbook publishers became alarmed that their
product might soon be rendered obsolete. To nip the problem in
the bud, they quickly entered into the educational software business, creating software that looked remarkably like their textbooks (and often referred users back to those books). In essence,
they took their textbooks, translated them to an electronic
medium, and added some bells and whistles to make their products look new and different. Over the years, they've upgraded
their software from a technical standpoint, creating "edutainment" that cleverly combines textbook teaching with game-style
action. These products may be enjoyable to use—kids like shoot-

ing verbs with an electronic gun as they scoot across the screen—but they're no more effective as learning tools than a teacher lecturing about grammar. Edutainment still doesn't let kids learn by doing, it's not tailored to a child's particular interest, and it doesn't put kids in complex situations that invite expectation failure. In fact it is mostly an attempt by the entertainment industry to capitalize on parents' desire for educational material for their kids.

On one front, there's not much you can do about this. You're not going to convince your school district to buy the right type of software, because there really isn't much to buy, nor are you going to loosen the textbook publishers' or entertainment industry's stranglehold on the market. What you can do, however, is distinguish the majority of bad educational software from the minority of good products, using the guidelines found later in this chapter.

Goal-Based Scenarios

In the interest of full disclosure, I should note that my company, Cognitive Arts, creates computer simulations for both schools and business. Though I can't claim to be a perfectly objective observer on this topic, I can assure you that I'm also not trying to sell you anything: You can't purchase Cognitive Arts computer simulations for use at home because we are mostly engaged in building simulations for corporations to train their employees. My purpose, therefore, is to give you a reasoned argument about the types of available software you should avoid and the types that will help you raise a smarter kid. To do so, let me describe two simulations we created for kids, one that's an exhibit at Chicago's Museum of Science & Industry geared for visitors of all ages (though primarily for children) and another that was designed for high school students.

Sickle Cell Counselor allows exhibit users to take on the role of counselors, advising a couple worried about having children because they're afraid their kids might be at risk for developing sickle cell anemia. Users gather information from the couple; test their blood in a simulated blood lab; consult experts such as a doctor, a geneticist, and a lab technician (who are recorded on video and can respond to a wide variety of user questions); calculate the risks; and advise the couple accordingly. The goal of this simulation isn't to learn about human biology but to figure out the couple's gene types. Users are motivated to help the couple make the right decision, and the simulation challenges them to resolve the situation.

Broadcast News is a more sophisticated simulation, allowing high school students to create their own television newscast. Incorporating a camera, VCR, and computer editing tools, Broadcast News helps users learn about history, economics, political science, and other subjects rather than train them to be journalists. Students have access to video production facilities and cobble together a newscast based on their own interviews, fact-checking, and other actions; they even anchor the newscasts themselves. The computer plays certain newsroom roles, assigning the student stories to cover, writing stories to be incorporated into the newscast, and so on. The rough draft of the story the student is assigned contains intentional errors of fact as well as less tangible errors (such as biased reporting)—errors that the student has to find and correct by interviewing experts (whose responses are videotaped and accessible), checking wire service copy, and asking questions. What motivates students is the desire to produce a first-class newscast. They receive copies of the newscast they create, and since they're the anchors, they want the tapes to look and sound professional.

Let's look at how these simulations conform to our learning model:

- **Diverse experiences.** Though simulations aren't the real thing, they come close enough that users feel as if they were advising the couple about the risk factors to their baby and as if they were producing a newscast. During this process, users find themselves in all sorts of unfamiliar and complex situations. While it would be nice if they could experience all these things in the real world, this simulated environment is a good laboratory in which to practice and take risks.
- **Reflection on and articulation of experience.** These programs encourage kids to think about what's just happened as well as to "talk" about it with an expert embedded into the simulation; they can ask questions about events and situations, request more information, and express confusion.
- **Expectation failure.** These simulations aren't easy. Students invariably make mistakes and take wrong paths as they attempt to resolve situations. In fact, the simulations are designed to lead users toward expectation failure; events unfold in such a way that kids make false assumptions that lead to mistakes. Once they realize they've made mistakes, they can ask experts questions or find information that will help them avoid making the same mistake twice.

Software Evaluation Checklist

As you decide which software titles to purchase for your child, don't fall for the sales pitches. Just because a CD-ROM has been endorsed by a national education association or promises to help your child become proficient at math, science, art, or writing doesn't mean that it's any better or any different than what you'd find in a library book. Don't evaluate software based on its graphics or because of the clever way it disguises information in the form of games kids like to play. Instead, rely on the following eight criteria:

- **Offers learning by doing experiences**. Look for software that requires your child to complete a task—a task that requires knowledge or skills worth learning. This means spotting the fakes: the software filled with sound and fury but signifying nothing beyond a book translated to a screen. Don't fall for software that requires kids to do lots of meaningless activities that resemble video arcade games. Doing means taking on a challenging task worth doing (as opposed to a game that's pure fun) and struggling a bit before completing it.

- **Presents problems before providing instructions.** The program should be sufficiently difficult that children encounter problems with it, struggle, and when they're struggling, receive instruction. This goes back to the concept of expectation failure; it's only when people are surprised that they can't solve a problem as they expected that they're receptive to helpful information. This represents just-in-time learning. Good software provides kids with help at the moment when they really need and want it.

- **Includes good stories.** Kids respond much better to information in the form of well-told, entertaining stories than dry facts delivered in standard, textbook fashion. Every expert in every field has wonderful stories to tell. Look for software that lets these experts tell stories cleverly, quickly (no more than one minute in length), and in response to a child's question. If the software is about gravity and the child is confused about the principle behind it, Sir Isaac Newton should be sitting under a tree telling the story about how an apple fell on his head rather than a boring professor lecturing about gravity's ups and downs.

- **Is child-centered.** With the best programs, kids control the software rather than the software controlling the kids. Avoid programs that tell users exactly what they should do and when. Programs can recommend directions, but software should give children as much freedom of choice as possible. By fostering exploratory learning, a good program allows different children to pursue different paths to achieve the same outcome. We routinely build simulations that accommodate different interests and learning styles. Some people like to ask lots of questions and gather information as they move forward. Others prefer to try things, fail, and try again without asking many questions. Programs that allow kids to follow their interests and instincts maximize their desire to explore and learn.

- **Allows graceful failure.** You've probably encountered computer programs that make users feel stupid when they make mistakes. There are computer games where a cartoonish figure blows a figurative raspberry at the user when he fails. There should be no stigma attached to failure. When expectations fail, the software should provide helpful choices in response to the failure. Ideally, the software should not be so difficult that its tasks are almost impossible for kids to complete; continuous frustration doesn't produce graceful failure.

- **Lets kids navigate their way to answers**. Don't purchase software that is pure instruction. The best software allows users to ask questions and receive reasonable answers; this question-and-answer process is a natural way to explore a subject. There are also times when kids don't know which questions to ask, and in these instances the program should allow children to search through the system to see what tools are available. It should clearly show them the menu of choices; they should be aware of what the information base is and the various ways they can access it.

- **Provides a test that is in the doing.** Some programs mimic the multiple choice tests and true-false quizzes of school; they seem designed to reassure parents that their educational software is holding children accountable for what they learn. Of course, they're just reinforcing the false notion that memorizing trivia is the essence of learning. Software should be designed in a way that moves children from one level to the next. Once they effectively complete a task, deal with a situation, or solve a problem, they are given a different and perhaps more difficult assignment. They automatically "pass" to the next level with success.

- **Is fun and fully engaging.** While all play and no work is bad, all work and no play is worse. Good software, no matter how educational, should have a strong element of fun. If your child finds a piece of software dry and boring, he won't learn anything from it. He needs to be fully engaged in what he's doing or he'll just go through the motions. If your child has trouble tearing himself away from the computer, if he is calling you to the computer to show whatever "cool" event is taking place, then the software meets this requirement.

Internet Opportunities

While there may not be a plethora of software that fits the criteria just established, the Internet offers children a variety of ways to learn and develop their areas of interest. You should purchase computers that can connect to the Internet relatively quickly, preventing your kids from being frustrated by slow connections and downloads. Beyond that, you need to encourage your children to explore the Internet by doing a few simple things:

1. When your child asks you a question, march over to the computer and say, "Let's see what we can find about this on the Internet."

2. Tell your child about Internet sites that dovetail with her area of interest.

3. Share in your child's excitement when she tells you what she discovered on the Internet; listen and let her show you what she's found.

Let me explain why all this is important now, and why it will be even more important in the near future. Presently the Internet is a valuable tool for exploratory learning. It's not just the ultimate library (although it is that). It's a place where one thing leads to another. You can start at one site and become interested in a link to a second site and find an even more exciting link to a third. Plus, it's not just blocks of information. While some sites remain mired in text, others are more imaginative, providing users with opportunities to ask questions, to talk to other people with like-minded interests, and even to solve a problem or navigate through different types of information.

In terms of smart kid traits, the Internet is ideally suited to fostering inquisitiveness. It engages children with ideas and opinions to be curious about the great diversity of the Internet, ensuring that not only will they find something related to an area of interest but that there will be a multiplicity of viewpoints about that area of interest.

Ultimately, the Internet will become a more experiential medium as simulations take the place of pure information. Instead of visiting a site that tells you about a linear accelerator, people will be able to run a simulated accelerator. Automobile manufacturers will have sites that will offer car enthusiasts a chance to design a concept car. There will be much more doing, which will lead to more diverse experiences, expectation failure, and true learning.

For now, however, it's still a worthwhile place to go when a question arises or information is needed. For example, imagine the subject of volcanoes comes up in a conversation or school report or from watching a movie. It won't take long to find out about the volcano that is currently exploding in Montserrat; your child can receive daily reports or make contact with scientists who are studying what is happening there and acquiring cutting-edge knowledge every day. A dry and nonchanging encyclopedia cannot easily compete with a medium that is continuously changing and offers the possibility of communication with others.

There's another important Internet issue for parents of bright children to consider. Smarter kids often feel like oddballs; they may even be viewed as such by other, duller children. The Internet demonstrates to them that there are others out there with the same interests, no matter how esoteric those interests might be. They can talk to these other kids, share their ideas, and generally feel as if they are part of a community. They may even learn about how they can turn their arcane interest into a career when they're older, fueling their ambition. Even better, sharing ideas and opinions with other like-minded kids motivates them to develop more knowledge and skills in their area of interest, to dig deeper and challenge themselves to learn more. In other words, it fosters gumption's stick-to-itiveness.

The Computer Alone Is Not the Solution

Computers by themselves can't raise smarter kids. I'm not making this observation facetiously, but in response to those who place too much faith in the power of computers as learning tools. The last thing I would want is my child spending ten hours each day in front of the computer. Earlier I recommended that kids have access to computer simulations in school. Once such simulations become available, it still wouldn't be a great idea for them to spend all their time on them. Ideally, the school day would be equally divided into three segments. After working at the computer, the kids would meet and discuss what happened during their simulations. This discussion is important, not simply because it conforms to our learning model (telling stories about one's experiences) but because it can help kids develop new interests or take their own interests in new directions. The one-on-one exchanges between peers—with the teacher acting as a facilitator rather than the font of all knowledge—capitalizes on children's innate desire to talk about what excites them. The final third of the day would be devoted to a real world activity that parallels the subject of the student's computer simulation. If someone did a simulation related to building things, the activity might involve spending some time as an intern in an architect's office.

Until schools wise up and incorporate this type of curriculum, you need to do what you can to set up a similar system at home. This means not allowing your child to spend every waking second on the computer. It means taking the time to listen to your child's stories about what happened when he was on the Internet or working on some program. And it means taking your kid out of the house to a real place where he can experience the same areas that interest him when he's on-line (it can be as simple as taking a child who loves animal-related programs to the zoo or someone who is interested in computer design to a graphic arts studio).

Above all else, don't make the same mistakes other parents make relative to computers. At one extreme are the parents who never use a computer and may not even know how to use one, yet expect their children to embrace this technology. You want your children to see you at the keyboard, looking eager and excited about the programs you're using and the sites you're exploring; they'll pick up on the behavior you're modeling. At the other extreme, don't feel that you have to "force" your children to become computer literate by making them take computer classes or insisting that they work on a computer program they find boring. Most children don't need any special instruction in how to use a computer; the interfaces are sufficiently simple that just spending a little time playing around with a program will allow them to get the hang of it. Learning to program, too, is no longer a particularly important skill for most kids.

Ideally, your child will use the computer with a goal in mind—not your goal but his own. He'll get on the Internet in search of a particular topic or site. He'll work on a program that helps him develop a skill or area of knowledge that's important to him; you won't have to nag him to do it. Or he might just play around. Playing around in an arena of knowledge and information can turn out to be much better experience than playing on a jungle gym. At the very least, your child will have an almost infinite variety of ways to exercise his mind.

14

Why You Need to Act Now

AS someone who loves learning, I hate what schools are doing to our children. I suspect that you hate it too. Like many parents, you may be upset by the despairing look on your child's face when you wake him in the morning and tell him it's time for school; feel frustrated when he tells you how boring school is, how the teacher doesn't like him, or how anxious he is about an upcoming test. Most of all, you may worry that school has robbed him of his natural love of learning. By early adolescence, so many formerly curious, intellectually adventurous children have been turned into incurious conformists. Even if they receive good grades, they demonstrate little enthusiasm or excitement about the subjects themselves.

This attitude is neither hormonal nor an adolescent act. It is the result of too many years studying uninteresting things in uninteresting ways.

This book will help you prevent your smarter child from being dumbed down by the school system. Instead of engaging in an unwitting conspiracy with the schools to make him an unthinking rule-follower, you now know that you can free him from their control. The analogy of deprogramming and mind control may be hyperbolic, but it raises an important issue: Schools exert a powerful influence on kids that few analyze or question. We may point out flaws in the system, but most of us accept its fundamental principles absolutely. This is why relatively few parents voice concern about a system that bores students to tears and comes down hard on kids who express original thoughts.

Whether purposefully or not, schools have done a good job of brainwashing us to believe that they're in the business of helping us raise smarter kids. In reality, they teach kids how to succeed in an artificial system that does not bode well for your children specifically and society in general. If this line of thought strikes you as alarmist, it's because our children are really in danger. It's easy to say, "This problem doesn't apply to my kid; he's only four," or "It's too late for my child; she's already in college."

It's never too early or too late to raise a smarter kid. You can have a significant impact on helping your child develop meaningful interests and skills, but only if you put aside your misconceptions about school and your own sense of powerlessness. I'd like to conclude with what the advertising people term "a call to action," explaining why it's so important for you to act now.

Two Alarming Trends

It's always been important for children to develop the six traits of smarter kids. Now, however, there are two compelling reasons for you to do everything possible to nurture this development.

First, the school system is more standardized than ever before. In the relatively recent past, it still had some give. There was room for idiosyncratic teachers who ignored or at least downplayed the curriculum. Students were given some leeway to pursue their interests through independent study courses and extracurricular activities. Elective courses outside the core curriculum—music, art, photography, and many others—were widely offered and provided real opportunities for students to pursue their interests.

Today, elective courses have been cut back for budgetary and, more significantly, for testing reasons. Schools have become obsessed with preparing students for the battery of standardized tests that are thrown at them. Teachers are driven to "cover all the material," to stick to the syllabus, to keep all classroom discussions focused on the topic at hand. The call for new standards has resulted in more regimentation, less flexibility, and more concern than ever with tests. There is very little room for students to pursue their individual interests or express ideas that are odd or unusual or deviate in any significant way from what the curriculum says these ideas should be. If you doubt the pressure schools are under to raise test scores, let me tell you about the Six Ps, the six factors that coalesce to maintain the educational status quo:

- Politicians—they put subtle (and sometimes not so subtle) pressure on the schools in their districts to boost test scores.
- Press—the media focus undue attention on scores, running banner headlines whenever scores rise or fall.
- Princeton #1—this is the Princeton that's home to the Educational Testing Service, which has a vested interest in preserving the standardized testing system.
- Princeton #2—this is Princeton University and all the colleges that slavishly use test scores as a determinant for who gets into their schools.

- Publishers—educational publishers have a vested interest in maintaining the current curriculum and publish textbooks that reflect this curriculum.
- Parents—many parents want their kids to be taught what they were taught in the same way they were taught; they are slaves to the educational tradition.

The second issue is that many kids are being funneled into fields for which they have little enthusiasm. As I've noted earlier, we live in a society where going to law, medical, or business school has become a reflexive response. Intelligent kids, especially, gravitate to these fields, convinced that at least they'll make good money and have a prestigious profession. In a world where there's so much uncertainty and change, these seem like "safe" careers. Unless you help your children discover and pursue their true interests and develop the gumption to resist societal pressures to play it safe, they may end up in jobs that make them miserable (or at best leave them as bored as they were in school).

Helping Your Child Become an Expert

Another compelling reason to work with your child in the ways I've described is that it will foster expertise, a prized commodity these days. In highly competitive fields, especially, just about everyone has an advanced degree and has achieved a certain level of competence. Expertise is a difference-maker; people who demonstrate true mastery of a needed skill are the ones who get ahead. It's not enough for your child to do what he's interested in; you want him to excel.

While every parent wants his child to "be the best he can be," it's not likely to happen if he doesn't intervene in his child's informal education. Schools teach students that to get ahead in the world, they should follow the same tactics that allowed them to get good grades: work mindlessly on what one was told to do. Unfortunately, being a grind will get them only so far in the real world. While there are some professions that reward following the rules and working hard, most success these days is predicated on traits such as creativity, gumption, verbal proficiency, and so on. Whether your child is going to work for herself or for someone else, you want her to develop expertise, and the way to do so is by developing the six traits.

Expertise is self-invention. In other words, people who are breakthrough thinkers in their fields and are responsible for pioneering new approaches and concepts have not followed prescribed paths. Their expertise is a result of their innovative thoughts and actions.

These traits are not going to develop—or they won't develop to the fullest extent possible—if you raise a rule-follower. Solid practitioners follow rules; experts rely on cases—sets of experiences that can be assessed and compared to other experiences. Great scientists don't follow the rules but do look for exceptions to the rule. They search for the disparate case—the one that breaks the rules—and start to make generalizations to explain why it is disparate.

You want your child to become familiar with "on-the-edge" cases. Experts typically deal with situations that others can't handle because they're so unusual or atypical; ordinary practitioners are perfectly capable of handling the normal, everyday cases. That's why you should encourage your child to develop a taste for the weird, the offbeat, and the unexpected. You want his eye to catch events that don't follow the script, to nurture his ability to spot the anomaly, reflect upon it, and articulate it. This is what experts do, and you should be helping him practice this skill.

You also need to expand the possibilities open to your child so that she can find a viable area in which to build expertise. Let's say your child's passionate interest is making up plays and having her dolls act them out. She dreams of becoming an actress. This is a nice dream, but it is not an easy career path, and few succeed at it. What you want to do is encourage her to start writing down her plays. As she develops writing skills, a variety of worlds will open up to her. It may be more important for her to write for the school paper or write a play for her friends than for her to concentrate on her English assignments. She might eventually look for jobs that require writing. You could encourage an interest in multimedia, where all sorts of new opportunities for writers are opening up. In truth, school won't help with too much of this, but the more you expand and direct her interest, the better her chances of finding work that she is good at and that matters to her.

Explicit Versus Implicit Knowledge

It is currently fashionable to say that knowledge is the new competitive advantage. There are parents who take this concept literally, pushing their children to memorize every fact and figure they can find. In fact, this type of knowledge is less important to learn than ever before. Computers make any bit of information we need to know available in seconds, and it's available to everyone. We've democratized the knowledge of facts and figures, and today the real opportunities exist in another realm.

Therefore, don't stuff your child full of facts. I know I've said this before, but it bears repeating, especially from the standpoint of developing expertise. If you're like most parents, you assume that the more your child knows, the more successful he'll be. In one sense, this is true, though not in the sense most people believe. The best airline pilots don't know the most facts about their planes. The best doctors haven't memorized every single fact and figure related to their area of specialty. What these experts do possess is implicit (or unconscious) knowledge as opposed to explicit (or conscious) knowledge. Expertise is about thinking quickly and effectively when faced with a complex situation. When we're in the car and suddenly skidding toward the edge of a cliff, our driving expertise allows us to steer and brake in such a way that we avoid being killed. When our boss is faced with a crisis, our expertise about handling complex situations helps us jump in and extricate him. None of this stuff is taught in the manuals because there are no manuals for life. It simply has to be lived. School does everything it can to keep kids away from real life and real experiences.

Keep all this in mind the next time you're tempted to fall in line with the school's thinking and insist that your child apply himself and memorize the periodic table or all the parts of a cell. This is not worth getting hung up on. If your child really is interested in science, it's a much better idea to help him find a summer job or unpaid internship in a place where he can do something with science: dissect things, mix stuff in test tubes, shoot particles at targets in an accelerator, and peer through telescopes and microscopes. This is where your child will develop implicit knowledge.

Don't Some Kids Develop the Six Traits of Smarter Kids Naturally?

Aren't some children just born with traits like verbal ability or inquisitiveness, and won't these traits blossom even if they're never taken on a trip, watch a ton of television, and are allowed to eat every meal at a fast-food restaurant? We all know very successful people who have developed implicit knowledge without their parents following the guidelines I've suggested here. They're the ones who have made their marks through sheer grit and determination and have overcome parents who put them down or ignored them and a school system that refused to let them pursue their interests.

But many of these successful adults have paid a price for their success. To overcome a lack of support from their parents, many of them have had to become so single-minded and narrowly focused that some other part of them never developed. As a result, they're workaholics, unable to form meaningful personal relationships, or they have compromised their values.

But let's look at this issue another way. Is there anything so wrong in wanting your child to grow up to become a good, decent person who achieves moderate success? Quite typically parents raise their children to do what they're told and always obey teachers, parents, and other authority figures; to please others first before considering their own needs. This may well lead to the creation of a well-adjusted member of society. A more likely scenario for very bright children, however, is that they'll rebel against regimentation. You need to be on their side when this happens, because their rebellion is against the conformity and acquiescence that will ultimately prevent them from becoming experts. If you don't support their refusal to fall in line with all the school's rules and regulations, they may never reach their potential and always struggle to be content with a life that they find moderately interesting and moderately successful at best.

Wouldn't it be preferable to raise an interesting, unusual child who isn't afraid to challenge authority figures, take risks, and fail, a child whose adult life reflects the intellectual passions of his inner life? An overarching parental attitude that helps achieve this goal is the following:

Nurture and support the "oddballness" of your child.

If you child is very verbal, displays gumption, or is highly inquisitive, she's going to be viewed as odd by others, especially by teachers and peers. If she discovers an unusual area of interest and pursues it with a certain obsessiveness or with unbridled creativity, she'll be considered strange. You need to defend your child's behaviors and encourage her despite what others say about her. When you're called in for a chat with the school counselor and he says he's concerned that your kid is disrupting class with her tangential questions or that she doesn't seem interested in the subject matter, you can't cave in. The last thing you should do is tell your daughter that she has to broaden her interests and must refrain from asking questions that challenge what the teacher believes. What you should do is find outlets for your daughter's interest and take time to answer (or, more appropriately, help her discover the answer for herself) all the questions bubbling inside her.

Certainly some odd behaviors cross the line and are socially unacceptable or symptomatic of a deeper problem, and I'm not suggesting you should support every bizarre action your child takes. What I am suggesting is that you recognize what makes your child distinctive and help your child develop this aspect rather than discourage it.

Kids don't develop meaningful career goals in a vacuum. If they lack the requisite variety of complex experiences, it's entirely possible that they'll fall into a career rather than consciously choose it based on their interests. John Greenleaf Whittier wrote, "Of all sad words of tongue and pen, the saddest are these: 'It might have been.'" One way to look at your role as parent is to help your children dream interesting dreams. You want to prevent your adult child from bitterly looking back and wishing he had pursued something that fascinated him. When I tell people that my son has a master's degree in transportation planning, their responses suggest that he's chosen an odd field and that they wonder how he could possibly have ended up there.

Perhaps because I turned him loose on the Paris Métro and let him explore the system.

I don't know if that single experience was the one that pushed him toward his future career. More likely, it was a series of transportation-related experiences combined with his own reflection, our discussions, and the expectation failures that occurred along the way. In any case, he is doing something he cares about passionately and at which he's very talented. Perhaps this would have happened if I had never raised him as I did, and that his fate from birth was to be a transportation planner. Still, it seems more likely that his "fate" would have been to choose a profession that was acceptable but not particularly exciting to him.

One Final Argument Against School to Keep in Mind

Don't let anyone convince you that you should give the school system another chance. This revisionism won't help you take action on behalf of your child. You may be tempted to decide that your child's school is different, that your kid has a great teacher. But keep the following facts in mind. Cheating is endemic to our schools, from grammar school all the way up through college. Kids are buying prewritten papers offered on the Internet and hire other students to take tests for them. You could even make an argument that the use of Cliffs Notes and taking courses designed to boost test scores are forms of cheating.

As long as kids feel the need to cheat on tests, the educational system is broken. In real life, very few people cheat. When adults are working at a job they care about, they want to know what they're doing wrong in order to improve. In any sort of apprenticeship, cheating is rare. If you're studying to be a master chef, you wouldn't ask someone to assemble your tiramisu because you want to pass the head chef's inspection. You would only be cheating yourself, since ultimately you're going to have to make this dessert on your own, and in cooking, as in other professions, the proof is in the pudding. Cheating becomes pointless if you have a meaningful goal and need to learn what is being taught to achieve it. Students cheat because the academic subject is meaningless to them. Tests aren't a diagnostic to measure learning but a way to succeed within the system. Though I know of no study on this issue, I would bet that the future writer doesn't cheat on his English literature essay but is much more likely to cheat on his math test. The future scientist may feel no compunction about purchasing a prewritten paper on Mark Twain but would never cheat on his chemistry test.

But wait, a defender of the system might protest, are you saying it's not important to learn about the history of our country, that our children don't need to know how to do mathematical equations, that it's not useful for them to learn a foreign language? This is exactly what I'm saying. Yes, it's important to learn basic reading, writing, and arithmetic, but these basics can be learned by the time children reach middle school. While it would be nice for students to learn all the subjects schools attempt to teach, we're fooling ourselves if we think they actually remember much if anything of what they're taught. Temporary learning is not learning. If knowledge isn't useful—if you don't apply what you've learned continuously—it's forgotten. On the other hand, when you learn something that matters to you and you use it constantly, it stays with you as long as you live.

Schools are subject-focused, and if they want students to learn, they need to become action-focused. They should be giving students complex tasks that are interesting to them. A student interested in design should work on a computer simulation that allows him to design a house. To carry out this task, the student would have to learn all sorts of subjects—math, economics, architectural history for a given locale, urban planning—but he would learn them in a usable context. At least some of the knowledge gleaned about each subject would remain with this student. The traditional academic subjects, therefore, should flow from the interesting, complex task rather than be taught in a way that's disconnected from any goal or interest.

Until schools allow students to learn by doing, every argument in favor of our current school system is bankrupt. You need to assume the role of your child's teacher today because it's going to be a long time before schools handle this role effectively.

It's Not Teachable, But It's Doable

You can't read this book to your child and expect it to make him smarter. You can't lecture him about the importance of diverse experiences and expectation failure and think it will have an impact. But there are things you can do. Some of the actions you can take are as easy as going on a trip with your child to taking him to an Ethiopian restaurant. Other actions will be more difficult.

Go into this with your eyes open. If you make the commitment to raise a smarter kid, recognize that you're going to encounter resistance, and not just from the school system. Most children are inherently conservative and will protest when you suggest new experiences. You have to play the bad guy sometimes and insist they work in a soup kitchen for a week or engage in some other unfamiliar experience. Similarly, you're going to have to swallow your pride and accept that it's okay if your child doesn't have the grades to get into Harvard or a similar type of institution. Encouraging your child to take a break, do what he likes, and not worry about receiving an A in a class is going to be difficult. When I told my son he needed a break from studying, he told me, "All the other kids in my class are working hard for top grades." I responded, "Well, you're pretty lucky because I won't make you do that." When the school calls to talk to you about your child's behavior, you have to guard against recidivism. When the principal informs you that your bright child (who tested so well) isn't performing up to his capacity, you need to fight against everything you've been taught about underachievers and accept underperformance as the best reaction your child can have to boring, irrelevant classes.

Perhaps the most difficult issue for parents involves spending enough time at home with their children. Two-parent working families have become the norm, and in most families it's asking a lot for one parent to stop working and stay home with the child, particularly since what matters is not just the first year of the child's life but every year until the child goes off to college (working part-time or in a job that provides sufficient flexibility for at least one parent to be home when the child is there can be a viable alternative). In fact, it's asking a lot for any parent— working or not—to spend the requisite time with a son or daughter. Kids can be tedious, annoying, and exasperating, usually in direct proportion to the amount of time you spend with them. After a hard day at the office, the last thing you might want to do is engage in a Socratic dialog with your surly child.

While I don't want to minimize the difficulty of doing what I'm suggesting, neither do I want to minimize the rewards. Specifically, your child will:

1. Have the courage of his convictions and pursue his goals with tremendous tenacity.
2. Be able to think on his feet, demonstrating a quick wit and having the ability to make a cogent and articulate argument.
3. Set his sights high, wanting to achieve great things and believing himself capable of doing so.
4. Create original ideas that push the boundaries.

5. Demonstrate a relentless curiosity, manifested by his desire to ask interesting questions and explore the answers.
6. Size up a situation quickly and accurately, cutting through the clutter and reasoning out effective solutions and strategies.

Nurturing gumption, verbal proficiency, ambition, creativity, inquisitiveness, and analytical ability is the most valuable gift you can offer your child. It may not help him earn great grades and citizenship awards or pave his way toward a traditional career path, but it will enable him to achieve his goals, work at what he's passionate about, and lead a fulfilling life. These might not be the measures by which school judges his success, but to a parent, it's the most meaningful report card of all.